Heartfelt Connections

Have Courageous, Honest, and Thoughtful Conversations with Yourself, God, and Others

Dezlee Hancock

Heartfelt Connections
Have Courageous, Honest, and Thoughtful Conversations
with Yourself, God, and Others

Inspired Legacy Publishing is a division of (DBA) Inspired Legacy, LLC
PO Box 900816
Sandy UT 84090-0816.

Changing Names & Medical Advice
Some names and identifying details have been changed
to protect the privacy of individuals.
This book is not intended as a substitute for the medical advice
of physicians. The reader should regularly consult a physician in
matters relating to his/her health and particularly with respect to any
symptoms that may require diagnosis or medical attention.

ISBN 979-8-9943758-1-5 (paperback)
ISBN 979-8-9943758-0-8 (hardcover)

Printed in the United States of America.

What People Are Saying

"Have you ever read a book and felt your whole life shift? Heartfelt Connections is that book! After studying human behavior for over thirty-five years, it's rare that I find a book about personal development that really moves me. Dezlee has created something truly soul-filling in the pages of this book."
—Laurie Hartley-Moore, Holistic Health Practitioner

"The lessons and lived experiences shared here gently invite you to take constructive steps toward the life you want and the relationships that truly nourish you. With spiritual insight and practical guidance, this book becomes a warm companion, showing how courageous, honest, and thoughtful words can reshape your world from the inside out."
—Gary L. Fretwell, #1 International Best-selling Author of: *The Magic of a Moment: Unlock the Potential in Every Moment and Unlocking the Magic: Your Daily Journal*

"Her words are invitations to creating a lifelong love story with one's self, as well as creating more meaningful relationships to those in your world. Heartfelt Connections is a journey, and a conversation, that I want to return to over and over again as the author reminds us, practice makes better."
—Sherry Lynn Campbell, Novelist, Children's Author and Storyteller

"This is a beautifully written, soul-nourishing book that lingers long after the final page. I could not put the book down. This is an example of truth and raw emotion that inspired me from the depths of my heart!"
—Deborah Wiener, Author, Speaker, Business Consultant, and Coach

"At some point in our lives, we will be faced with difficult conversations, either with family members, professionals, or both. This is a book I will keep close by and reflect on often. I highly recommend!"
—Wendy L Hooton- Author, *Big People Don't Pee in the Park: A Mother and Son's Journey with Down Syndrome*, Down Syndrome Advocate, Speaker

"Everyone can benefit from Heartfelt Connections. Dezlee's insights and experiences with a better way of communicating will change your life."
—Betsy Seamons, LCSW

"Though we may have many difficult relationships to work on, this book is one of the best tools to create a positive outcome. Heartfelt Connections is the worldview solution to coming together as a human race."
—Lisa Sitze, #1 International Best-selling Author of *Facing Your Demons*

"I recommend this book for ANYONE. We all can use this book to break down our own barriers and improve our relationships with one Courageous, Honest, and Thoughtful conversation at a time! The world needs Dezlee's book!"
—Sanya Watkins, Writer, Story Coach, Inspired Writer

"Dezlee Hancock invites the reader to see conversations in a fresh, inspiring way that transforms communication. Since implementing her CHAT formula, I've seen a significant improvement in my ability to communicate more deeply with my family, making basic conversations more meaningful and effective. I recommend this book to everyone who wants to uplevel their relationships, whether at work, at home, or in the community."
—Karen Munson, Author of the *God Given Grit* series

"This is the kind of book that reminds you of who you want to be—both for yourself and the people you love. It's heartfelt, practical, faith-anchored, and full of light."
—Lauri Mackey, Authoress of *Positivity Happens*

For all the hearts yearning to find connection

Contents

Of All the Things She Could Have Said

It was a typical school morning—four kids to wrangle, four clocks ticking, and one mom with a self-imposed rulebook about being on time. Because if everything was on time, then everything was right. And if everything was right, then I was doing a good job. There was no gray area. You. Just. Were. Not. Late. Not in my world!

All four of my kids—from ages five to fifteen—attended different schools, which was a special kind of torture for someone with a time obsession. Everyone knew the routine: get ready, eat breakfast, find your backpack, and march out the door like a well-oiled machine. Everything was just fine—unless someone broke formation. Then it all unraveled.

That morning, it was my oldest daughter, Karlie. Eleven years old and planted in front of the bathroom mirror, but not brushing her teeth or fixing her hair. She was picking at her pimples. And not flying out the door to catch the bus.

"What are you doing?" I snapped, my voice rising. "Don't you know it's time to leave? I'm not driving you to school if you miss the bus!" I didn't let her answer. I didn't even stop to breathe.

That's when she turned away from the mirror, raised her hands to her face, and like a dragon spewing fire, hurled out the two ugliest words on the planet:

"Shut. Up!"

Then she bolted. Down the stairs. Out the door.

"What?" I said out loud—to myself, as no one was around. "What did she just say?"

I stood there frozen, too stunned and shocked to even move. "Did she really just say *those* words?" I muttered. I've never had any of my kids say those words to me. *I can't believe it,* I thought. Here's why: those words were the ultimate crime in our house. Even the hint of "shut up" would get someone put in time-out jail. I'd never used that phrase; I detested it. And it wasn't just that she said it—it was that she knew what it meant.

My own daughter! Of all the things she could have said . . .

You may be thinking, what's the big deal? People say those words all the time. I know—I hear them. But just because something is common doesn't mean it's not toxic. And in our home, those two words were the ultimate dealbreaker.

I dragged my heavy body and aching heart to the couch, fully intending to cry. A well of tears was already rising. I wanted to blame someone—anyone—for what had just happened. Surely this wasn't my fault. Right? But just as the flood of tears came, so did something else—clarity.

This wasn't just about Karlie blurting out those two forbidden words. It was about me. I'd been trying to control my life from the neck up—with logic, routine, and sheer force of will—while leaving out kindness, compassion, and understanding. For far too long, my conversations had reflected feelings of burnout, disconnection, and emptiness.

The incident with my daughter was the straw that broke the camel's back. Devastated that my relationship with her had reached this point, I realized that my everyday routines had become heavy and exhausting, marked by contentious conversations about money, kid problems, cell phones, things breaking down, running a business, and—of course—being on time. Life was not what I thought it would be, and I was unable to control it. I didn't want to be in this deep, dark hole that I had dug for myself. But here I was.

This was my reality, and I didn't want to feel any more regret about things I said when I simply was not thinking about my words! I wanted to be understood, and I wanted to understand. I needed to live more deeply and that meant more heart and soul to go along with my head. I knew creating better conversations would be the key to enjoying my relationships *because they mattered to me*.

After that transformational altercation, I changed my words, my messages, and my heart. My relationships got better. Life got better. I was astounded at how I was creating a better life *with my words*. Sometimes I would be so amazed at the things that would happen . . . all because of how I *used* my words! Conversations weren't just a bunch of syllables meshed together anymore. They became connecting moments of meaningful relationships and a life worth enjoying. While it wasn't quick or convenient, it has been worth every moment of mastering my thoughts and my words. Do I still like to be on time? Oh, you betcha! But now I am enjoying greater results, without being demanding, grouchy, or controlling the people around me.

For a long time after my big breakthrough, I kept these profound, life-changing experiences to myself. I hesitated to put out there what had come to my heart and soul. I can't deny that I've had defining, spiritual moments—experiences that taught me so much about the importance of connecting hearts and finding a better way of doing things. God helped me on this journey to a more abundant life by showing me how to connect hearts. In His own way, He let me know that these experiences weren't just for me, but for others, too, and not sharing them would be selfish.

I'm also aware that while this single conversation is what set me on the path to writing this book, it might seem trivial compared to the weight of deeper wounds you, dear reader, may have experienced—abuse, divorce, betrayal, racism, or other forms of pain and hate. Please know that I recognize life carries unique burdens for each of us. Though I may not address every hardship individually, my hope is that this book becomes a starting point—a gentle step toward healing, peace, and the life you truly desire.

Ultimately, this book moves far beyond those two words spoken by my daughter and into the deeper relationships we need to have with ourselves, with God, and with others.

From Mess to Message

Since then, I've felt a deep sense of responsibility—along with a strong sense of purpose—to share what I've been given. Whenever I do, I can't help but speak with passion and joy because of the profound impact it's had on my life. As Maya Angelou said, "When you learn, teach. When you get, give."

What began as a personal goal to connect more deeply with Karlie and the rest of my family quickly turned into something much bigger. I found I couldn't just watch from the sidelines as people hurt each other with their words. It was too painful!

At first, I did everything I could within my small circle: family, friends, coworkers. But then I began encountering strangers—and without even planning to—I found myself speaking up, offering insights to help guide their conversations. In group settings, I shared what I'd learned about courageous, honest, and thoughtful dialogue. People were skeptical at first, then curious—excited even—by the possibility of changing their world.

Soon, people began asking regularly for help in healing relationships and resolving conflict through words. I found myself giving advice that didn't feel like my own but inspired by God.

Life has a way of bringing lessons, purpose, and growth back around to us, if we're open enough to let it happen. I knew it was my spiritual experiences that had led me to this place. Even writing about them brings emotions to the surface. With God's help, I've come to a deeper understanding of how impactful our words are in how we treat one another. I have been blessed—and continue to be blessed—to have the life I was yearning for so long ago.

This book is an invitation to open your heart through conversations grounded in courage, honesty, and thoughtfulness. It challenges us to move beyond surface-level talk and step into dialogue that creates a real connection. True conversation takes bravery, the courage to let go of defensiveness, the need to be right, and the fear of vulnerability.

If we want deeper, more meaningful relationships, we must lower our walls, soften our hearts, and speak with intention. You'll discover that words are powerful, and when chosen with care, they become a form of art that can heal, uplift, and transform.

Through this journey, you'll explore what it means to love yourself, how heart-led conversations can change lives, and why the color purple symbolizes connection with yourself, with God, and with others. Using the Purple CHAT approach, you'll walk through four steps: (1) becoming a better you, (2) creating a better message, (3) choosing better words, and (4) showing up as your best self.

If you are tired of avoiding conversations, this book is for you. If conversations make you uncomfortable, this book is for you. If you regret certain conversations you've had in the past, this book is for you. If you struggle with how to talk to yourself, this book is for you. If you want better relationships with a loved one . . . or anyone, this book is for you. If you want to make a positive impact in your workplace and stop having contentious conversations, this book is for you.

If you are dreading having a certain conversation . . . yes, of course, this book is for you!

Learn how to:

- Take responsibility for your happiness.
- Talk to yourself like a best friend.

- Value and love yourself like never before.
- Recognize that God is the beginning of all relationships and will help you connect hearts.
- Gain confidence in talking with other people.
- Have those hard conversations you want to avoid.
- Discover more meaning in life through the relationships that matter most.
- Show up for people and make an unforgettable difference in their lives.

You can wake up each morning filled with hope and enthusiasm for what the day will bring. With these discoveries, you can climb that mountain that's been blocking your view of what life truly has to offer. I invite you to experience life as a blessing, not just a job or a duty. Embracing courageous, honest, and thoughtful conversations is one of the most valuable investments you can make. These moments will help you find, gather, and strengthen the bonds that mean the most.

In the end, when everything else fades, it will be the depth of connection and love you cultivated in your relationships that reveals the life you've lived.

Welcome to this life-changing journey. You are courageous for wanting something better—for yourself and your relationships.

Let's get started.

PART I: BETTER YOU

Open Your Mind

"Those who cannot change their minds
cannot change anything."
—George Bernard Shaw

If Only . . .
Discovering Something Different

"Don't go through life, grow through life."
—Eric Butterworth

Y ou need something to change. Life shouldn't feel this hard, be so draining, or overwhelming. If *only* it could be different . . .

Have you ever caught yourself thinking, *If only things were different . . .*? If only I had more time or money. If only my spouse would change or my kids would do what I say. And of course, if only I looked different. I know that place well—it feels like standing on the outer edges of your own life, waiting for someone or something to make it better. As much as we want to believe that those things would make our lives better, they won't. No "if" will ever be enough. Real change doesn't begin when circumstances shift; it begins when *we* do. And it starts with the conversations we choose to have with ourselves, with others, and with God.

The path to a more meaningful life is self-change, self-discovery and self-love. When we nurture that inner relationship, something powerful happens. We begin to connect more deeply with others, and the world that once felt heavy and overwhelming starts to feel richer, lighter, more hopeful, and full of possibility.

I've learned this: change your inner conversation, and you change your outer world.

Our lives are made up of conversations, all day, every day, with ourselves and others. They can't be avoided. They happen first thing in the morning when our eyes pop open and our feet hit the ground until we find our solace in sleep. We often think communication only happens when we speak, but we're always expressing something, simply by being.

Our body speaks too. Eye contact or the lack of it, facial expressions, posture, pace, how we enter or leave a room, even how we sit in a chair; these are conversations. Even silence communicates something. As humans, we cannot *not* communicate. And these ongoing exchanges shape who we are, and the society we live in.

After the painful experience with my daughter—when my world seemed to fall apart—I found a chance to rebuild, this time with better intentions and a lot more thoughtfulness.

I came to realize that the "thing" that needed to be different was not something outside of me but *within* me. What was missing was a genuine, heartfelt connection, and for that to happen, it required courage to stop hiding behind my words and start leading with my heart. That's not easy. As humans, we're wired to protect our hearts to avoid pain and being uncomfortable, but I've learned that this way of living often comes at a cost, not just to those around us, but to our own sense of connection and belonging.

Over time, I saw how that disconnection went even deeper. It wasn't just affecting my relationships with others; it was weakening the bond I had with myself and with God. I had to face a hard truth: I had been focusing on routines, being on time, being right. But in doing so, I had lost sight of people, relationships, and simple thoughtfulness.

This journey has been humbling. But it's also been holy and sacred. Because every time I choose to lead with my heart, I feel a little closer to the person I was always meant to be.

Learning Deeper Connection

So what about this thing called connection? I knew I needed to delve into it more. Connecting is not the same for everyone. While we all have different wants, needs, and ideas, one truth remains: connection is a basic human need.[1] Psychology confirms what our hearts already know—our well-being depends on it. True connection brings us a feeling of closeness and belonging with others and a sense of identity with God, which we need not just to survive, but to truly thrive.

At our core, we long to be seen, heard, and wanted—physically, emotionally, and spiritually. And how do we express that? Through our conversations, both verbally and nonverbally. Yet in today's world, genuine connection is more challenging than ever. Not only with others but with ourselves.

---

[1] Kerr, Natalie, and Jaime Kurtz, "Our New Social Life: Science-Backed Strategies for Creating Meaningful Connection," Oxford Academic, (New York, 2025; online ed., 21 Nov. 2024), https://doi.org/10.1093/oso/9780197749951.001.0001, accessed 27 Sept. 2025.

I eventually realized that real connection—and real change—meant facing the endless list of "ifs" I had been storing in my head and believing. I made the decision to shift my thinking. But I soon discovered reality: old habits don't give up easily. They're comfortable. Familiar. They like to linger. But heartfelt connection required the shift, because the "ifs" kept my heart from being all in.

I knew a good place to begin was with my husband. I loved him—and yes, I'll say it—his sexy legs. (He's a tennis player, if you're wondering.) He was and is the ultimate gentleman. We shared the same goals in life and wanted the best for our family. But our conversations? They were tense. Same vision, different approaches. Sound familiar?

One day, Clark and I found ourselves alone in the kitchen, a rarity with kids around. The subject of buying a car came up again. Not just any car, but a rumbling orange Camaro he'd had his eye on. To me, it felt extravagant, even a little ridiculous. Yep, my head jumped in, leading without heart.

But this time was different. I paused, looked him in the eyes, and let go of needing to be right. I decided to truly see it from his point of view. He worked hard, harder than anyone I knew. And if he wanted to enjoy something just for himself, a little thrill beyond the family van, why not?

To Clark, that car was more than transportation. It was joy. Freedom. Life on wheels. My brain didn't get it, but my heart did. I realized the real decision wasn't about money or logic; it was about connection. And letting go of contention.

"Hey," I said, holding his gaze and steadying my voice, "I want you to have the car."

Clark froze. Blinked. He looked like a kid who'd been handed a giant bag of candy, unsure if it was real. I could feel something shift in that moment. I had stepped off the battlefield and into a new world.

Sure enough, within a month he was cruising down the road in that Camaro, listening to the music *loud,* while being on cloud nine. And the part I loved most? The way he smiled with his beautiful blue eyes.

Carefully Choosing Words Creates Miracles

Over time, with better conversations, my husband and I began to learn how to work together instead of against each other. We started listening, not only to respond, but to care more deeply about the message. Little by little, our conversations shifted from routine exchanges to moments of real connection. Understanding began to flow again. Life started to feel different.

We also had to face something simple but powerful: we are two different people, with two different perspectives, and that's okay. What mattered most was choosing to grow together.

Real World Problems

Of course, it wasn't just at home. The real world was just as hard, maybe harder. Everywhere I went, I was bombarded by conflicting voices, strong opinions, and loud judgments. I felt overwhelmed, defensive, and sometimes just . . . tired. It's hard to stay connected in a world so full of noise.

That inner struggle doesn't stay inside. It shows up in our conversations and relationships. If we want to feel whole again, if we want to move forward with purpose, we need to find our way out of the chaos and back into meaningful connection.

Why CHATs

I've learned that my most powerful conversations happen when I show up with three qualities: courage, honesty, and thoughtfulness. These three always invite others in, along with values like truth, kindness, and goodness.

That's what led to the idea of **CHATs**: *Courageous, Honest, And Thoughtful.*

It's more than an acronym. It's a way to remember that talking isn't just talking; it's an opportunity to connect deeply with yourself, and the world around you.

Since embracing this approach, I've seen how these qualities can elevate not just conversations, but hearts, including transforming my own.

Why Purple?

CHATs became such a turning point in my life when I stopped waiting for conversations to magically improve and started showing up differently—intentionally. Through Courageous, Honest, And Thoughtful conversations, I rebuilt relationships I thought were beyond repair. And somewhere along the way, the chaos around me faded. What remained was a meaningful, sacred journey.

That's when the color purple showed up in my life, not just as a shade, but a symbol. Purple stands for courage, sacrifice, honor, and unity. It's a color that bridges opposites. In a divided world of red and blue, black and white, purple brings hearts together.

Purple CHATs are conversations of the heart. They're not about winning an argument. They're about laying down ego for the greater good. They're about connection over correction, healing over hostility, peace over pride.

And something beautiful happens when we choose that kind of courage.

Having the Hard Conversations

Within just a few months of practicing courageous, honest, and thoughtful conversations, something began to shift in me. It felt like sunlight breaking through the clouds, giving me hope and encouragement as it gently warmed my soul. What began as an experiment soon became a way of life. Purple CHATs weren't just about better communication; they were reshaping the very fabric of my days. I was on my way to heartfelt connections.

I took a life-changing parenting class—more than once—and used what I learned in every role: mother, wife, friend, business owner. I practiced these new ways on my husband and kids, and they began to shift too.

It didn't stop there. The more I leaned into Purple CHATs, the more light and love filled my life. Sometimes, it felt like that elusive magic I'd been looking for! And I began to truly see how abundant my life had become, not because of external success, but because of the relationships and experiences that filled my soul.

As I was going through my own healing, I couldn't help but notice the world around me, people caught in painful, destructive struggles born out of careless conversations. You've likely seen it too: how words, instead of bringing understanding, so often bring division and hurt.

Somewhere along the way, we've lost the art of truly communicating which includes listening. Instead of being intentional with how we speak to one another, the focus has shifted. Too often, we want to be heard but don't want to put in the effort to hear what is being said. We don't aim for understanding; we aim to be right.

I heard it all the time from my kids, friends, and even strangers: "I hate talking to people. I'm done with conversations." And honestly, I could see why. Interactions had become hollow and careless. People seemed unaware, or uninterested, in the impact of their words. They'd left their hearts out of it.

But I knew something different was possible. I had seen it. Felt it. Lived it.

I felt like a healthy eater in a junk food world, ready to shout, "There's a better way!" Or a marathon runner watching people trip over their own feet. A conversation geek who wanted to clear her throat and say, "You know . . . if you said that a little differently, you might get a better result."

Why the Journey of Change Is Important

Every night, we can witness on television the heartbreaking consequences of poor communication: families torn apart, schools full of tension instead of trust, chaos instead of clarity, and a sharp rise in mental health crises. But I've also seen healing. And I believe we can turn things around, one heartfelt conversation at a time.

Yes, we all have "IFs" in life. But don't stay stuck in them. Having heartfelt connections with yourself will give you the courage to step into a different kind of life, one that isn't held hostage by your circumstances. Learn. Discover. Change. Love. This is your invitation to begin.

Purple CHAT Questions:
1. What are the IFs in my life?
2. Can I change any of them by changing myself?
3. When was the last time I discovered something new and impactful?

— 2 —

It's About You . . .
But Not About You

*"So this, I believe, is the central question
upon which all creative living hinges:
Do you have the courage to bring forth the
treasures that are hidden within you?"*
—Elizabeth Gilbert

Let's get real. There are days when people drive us crazy. Some people are difficult. Some are just annoying. But we're all human, and relationships come with conflict, tension, and a lot of figuring it out.

This chapter is about recognizing that, while conversations involve other people, the work begins with you. It's about learning to pause, reflect, and take responsibility for how you choose to interact with people.

Most of us weren't taught how to speak from the heart. We learned to defend, protect, blame, or shut down. We don't always realize how much of our inner pain leaks into our words, or how much our words impact others, and ourselves.

Caroline is one of those rare souls whose light seems to shine wherever she goes. With a warm smile that never fades—even from a hospital bed—she's the first to ask how *you* are doing, even as she quietly faces her own battles. She's walked through cancer with grace, always more concerned about others than herself. She listens deeply, gives freely, and offers help without hesitation. Caroline is loving, generous, talented, resourceful, and a true friend.

You may know someone like Caroline. Many of us do. But what most people didn't see was the lifelong struggle behind her smile.

Caroline grew up wanting to do the "right" things. She dreamed of a loving family, a life filled with faith, and a heart open to serving others. And she did all those things, until, piece by piece, it fell apart. Her most important relationships began to unravel, and the connections she had poured herself into slowly faded. At fifty-five, she found herself heartbroken and alone, unsure how things had come to this, feeling embittered, disempowered.

I was honored to stand beside her during those painful years. I listened as she shared her sorrow and fears, I hugged her through tears, and sat with her in moments when she wondered if she could go on. We spent hours having those *Purple CHATs*—conversations filled with Courage, Honesty, And Thoughtfulness. They were hard. They were healing. And they were necessary.

Caroline began to realize something she had never been taught: that loving yourself is not selfish and that true peace doesn't come from endlessly giving to others; it begins by connecting deeply with yourself. For so long, she had believed that thinking of herself *was* wrong and that her worth was tied to how much she could do for others. But in the process, she had emptied herself . . . completely.

When Caroline discovered the power of self-love, her heartache started to change. She began to understand that loving herself isn't selfish; it's essential. Slowly, with hesitation, she started saying "yes" when others offered her help. She learned to rest. To recharge. To receive. And she discovered something beautiful: she mattered too.

Caroline had always shown up for others. Now, she was learning to show up for herself. And it changed everything. As she connected with her own heart, she began to heal. And in turn, she reconnected with others in more meaningful ways. Her family noticed. Her friends noticed. Even she noticed.

This chapter is about finding that space within ourselves—the place where healing and connection begin. Too often, we think we have to fix everything else or make life perfect for everyone before we're allowed to take care of ourselves. But what if the opposite is true? What if the best thing we can do for those we love is to become whole ourselves?

Today, Caroline is still giving—because that's who she is—but she's also learning to receive. She's finding peace in the balance. Her life now holds more joy, more wholeness, and a deeper sense of connection, not just with others, but with herself and with God.

When Your Topics of Conversation Leave You Out

There's a lesson here for all of us. Like Caroline, many of us have a hard time thinking about ourselves, let alone the thought of loving and appreciating who we are. We ignore all that's going on inside of us, hoping that we can still be whole. But very few things work that way if they are pushed aside. A car can't run without gas, a plant will die without water, and cell phones stop working if not recharged. We too can't thrive without tending to our own hearts.

You're not alone in this. So many of us were taught that being selfless meant forgetting ourselves entirely. But there's a difference between selflessness and self-neglect. You matter. Your heart matters. Your healing matters.

So pause. Breathe. Listen to what's going on inside you. Love yourself, not because it's indulgent, but because it's the foundation of every meaningful relationship you'll ever have.

Caroline's journey is one of courage, awakening, and love. And it reminds us: our best life comes from within.

So now the questions are: *Are you nurturing yourself? Are you growing the person within—the one who shows up for others, for God, and for yourself?*

The topic of "you" or us is an interesting one and is often misunderstood. I've found two common beliefs that shape how we think and treat ourselves.

One comes from a Christian belief; while it has good intentions, it is most often misunderstood and applied. It teaches that thinking of yourself at all is selfish, even sinful. According to this view, your desires and needs should be completely ignored for the sake of others. The result? Many people put on a smile and lose themselves in the name of love.

Interestingly enough, the other philosophy is the polar opposite of the first, and it comes from a worldly perspective. This mindset is all about one person, and that is you. Chase what you want. Go out there and get all you can because you deserve it all. This way of thinking leads to an ego and behaviors of entitlement. You gain the world but lose connection.

Certainly, there has to be a middle ground. Are our only choices to lose ourselves for the sake of others or to find ourselves but lose others? Ugh! I don't like either one.

I believe there's another way. It's one we rarely reference in our daily lives; yet, it's woven into one of the greatest spiritual and moral truths ever given: **"Love your neighbor as yourself."**

It doesn't say *instead of* yourself.

It doesn't say *more than* yourself.

It says *as* yourself.

While this philosophy is not new to any of us, fully understanding and living it might be new. This approach towards "you" includes you *and* others. It's not saying one is more important than the other. The problem is that oftentimes we may hear "love your neighbor," but then start to fade out when it comes to ourselves. Like Caroline, we emphasize the first part and disregard the second half.

We do this when we:

- Give compliments to others, but then we tear ourselves down.
- Tell a struggling family member that they are loved, but then we can't say that to ourselves.
- Help a neighbor, but we can't ask for help ourselves when needed.
- Have compassion for a friend who is struggling, but then we beat ourselves up for the mistakes we have made.
- And the list goes on and on.

Why can we do good things for others, but we can't do them for ourselves?

This is why, when I say it's about you, but not about you, I truly mean it. You must start with yourself, *then* go serve your neighbor (and then it's not about you but your neighbor). It must start with you because you may be great, like Caroline, at loving other people, but it is imperative that you do the same for yourself. You can't forget that part, "yourself." Loving yourself comes first, so that you can do a good job of loving your neighbor.

The most important thing to recognize is the balance–that you and your neighbor are both important. You are not being selfish by thinking of and taking care of yourself. You are actually thinking of your neighbor too.

How to Love Yourself

This isn't about self-centeredness; it's about self-awareness. It's about recognizing that you have immense value and are worthy of care, compassion, and love. And when you begin to live from that place, you can give freely, without resentment, without burnout, and without losing who you are. The world doesn't need more people running on empty or running over everyone in their path. It needs more people anchored in love, while starting with the love they show themselves.

So here is the next question: *How are you doing when it comes to loving yourself?*

If you are uncomfortable with this question, you are not alone. Most of us don't even know how to answer this question, let alone be honest about it! But I look around and see people quietly falling apart–like Caroline once did–not because they're weak, but because they're carrying too much. Too much hurt, too much anger, resentment, loneliness, sadness, and shame can fill us up until we feel like we're barely staying afloat.

Resentment: A Natural Outcome of Overgiving

There's a quote that comes to mind: "A ship doesn't sink because of the water around it. It sinks because of the water that gets in it." — Unknown. Life definitely tosses buckets of water inside our ship. Things like pain, challenges, disappointment, and self-doubt are inevitable. We need to be tending to what is coming on board and bail the weight of it out so it doesn't sink us!

Loving yourself doesn't mean ignoring others. It means recognizing that *you* matter too. Because when we neglect that truth, our ship takes on too much, and eventually, it may go under. So, how do we become mindful if there is too much water in our boat?

The problem is when we give service in the name of love and obligation, but carry it out with resentment and anger, it festers. Do you feel resentful of the people you are giving to and serving in your life? That is a big, red flag. You're ignoring the water that will sink your ship. Service is wonderful, and I believe necessary to a fulfilling life, but *not* at the expense of your boat sinking. What good is a sunken ship?

This is where Purple CHATs come in, and it starts with us—*ourselves*.

- **Be Courageous** enough to recognize and feel emotions that you have buried or ignored. These could be both negative *and* positive ones. Studies show it's very powerful to write them out for clarity so that you truly recognize them.
- **Be Honest** with those feelings. You are the only one who knows your feelings. Now is the time to have integrity with yourself. Tell yourself the truth.
- **Be Thoughtful** when choosing the words you will say to yourself as you acknowledge your emotions. This will require new thought patterns that include compassion and understanding.

During her most trying times, I would often ask Caroline, "What would a 'loving Caroline' say to you right now?"

She would pause, and I could see the realization wash over her. She knew exactly what a loving Caroline would say because she had always known how to show compassion, kindness, and encouragement to others. What she hadn't realized was that she needed to offer that same love to herself.

It wasn't about becoming someone new. It was about turning the love she so freely gave to others . . . to herself.

The Biggest Win-Win

Loving ourselves makes life so much easier, and here is why. When we love ourselves, we are showing respect and appreciation for who we are, which in turn helps bring a sense of peace and goodness to our lives. This sense of peace and goodness benefits us with a greater satisfaction with life and changes our perspective of the world around us for good.

Loving ourselves is a win-win for everybody. "Love your neighbor" is a common theme in the world's major religions. In the Jewish and Christian scriptures of the Torah (early pages of the Bible), it states specifically to "love your neighbor as yourself." Hindu writings teach, "This is the sum of duty, do naught unto others what you would not have them to do to you." The Qur'an states, "Do good to those in need, neighbors who are near, neighbors who are strangers . . ." Jesus taught self-love as the second greatest commandment. First, to love God, and then to love your neighbor as yourself.

Self-love is the act of connecting yourself to your heart. It is like coming home to yourself and making that homecoming warm and welcoming. When we are connected to our own hearts, there is nothing better. It creates peace, love, and security within us, no matter what storms rage outside.

How Is Your Heart?

Some people may be confused by the phrase self-love, not having given thought to their own hearts. We have a heart, but how is our heart when it comes to genuine concern and love towards ourselves? I know plenty of people who have a hard heart towards themselves. They judge themselves harshly and constantly. They cannot say a single good word about themselves. Just because we have a heart does not mean it is serving us in the best way. You may have heard the term "hard-heartedness." This is a term that is often used in reference to others, but it begins with our feelings inside of us, our heart.

I invite you to learn how to *be* at home with *you*rself, not a stranger to yourself.

Why Loving Yourself Is Important?

If we do the work to truly love ourselves, we free up space we once used for battling against ourselves. Not only does it create peace and joy, but it also creates more room for loving others.

Hopefully, you can see the importance of starting with you. As you connect your heart with yourself, connecting with others becomes so much easier and satisfying. It will change your life! How you think about and love yourself is an important life skill in helping you find the fulfilling life you want and are capable of creating. It is like "seeing" from the inside out. It starts with the conversations you have about yourself, with yourself, and then looking outside at the world around you from a healthy place.

Purple CHAT Questions:

1. What would a loving me say to me?
2. Am I just as important as my neighbor?
3. Can I love myself and others at the same time?

Say Cheese!
Being Responsible
for Your Own Happiness

*"Do not set aside your happiness. Do not
wait to be happy in the future.
The best time to be happy is always now."*
—Roy T. Bennett

One of the first conversations we need to have with ourselves and get right is the one about our very own happiness. It's important that this topic not be overlooked because it lays the foundation for the rest of the work necessary for us to engage in Purple CHATs. It can be hard to lay claim to our own happiness, and yet it is vital.

It wasn't the best of times. As a seventh grader at Mesa Jr. High School, I was a typical kid, except for one thing. I had severe acne. Now you may say that a lot of kids that age have that puberty-growing-up-acne. But not me. Oh no, no one had acne like me. Mine was severe, and to make matters worse, my face turned intensely red from the medicine I was putting on it to try to control it. Oh, and it didn't help that I had crooked teeth and a big space between my two front teeth! Did I mention that I had no friends? People would say they were my friends, but somehow I was always alone when eating lunch and walking home after school.

Not being one to whine or be dramatic, I just did me. *Me against the world.* I guess I couldn't say that because I did have a great family, who absolutely accepted me as me, and loved me. My parents both had college degrees and full-time careers. My dad worked for the city of Mesa, and my mom was a nurse. We were, back then, a normal, middle-class family who ate dinner together every night and went to church on Sundays. There were seven kids, and we loved each other, worked together, and fought together. Traveling in the yellow truck and camper to family reunions *was* the best of times.

I was the second child with a sister just fifteen months older than me. Close in age, that put us close in grades at school. I was known as "Sharanette's younger sister." It seemed like that was my name. I loved my sister, but here was the dilemma: her skin was blemish-free, like a porcelain doll, and her teeth were perfectly straight. I am not kidding! Since she was so beautiful, I heard all about it. My parents were aware of my issues with my face and teeth, but they were not aware of how I was dealing with it on the inside. After all, they had seven kids!

One day, just before school ended, my teacher came over to my desk and handed me my school picture packet. Then she put her arm around my shoulders and gave me a little squeeze, you know, the kind that says, "hey, hang in there."

I didn't have much time to think about that squeeze, except that it was out of the ordinary, because the bell rang and everybody headed out the door. The classroom door led right out to the sidewalk, and kids started walking home. Just as I was about to head home by myself, a girl from my class walked up to me and asked if she could see my school picture. Without hesitating, I pulled out the picture and turned it around for her to see.

"Oh," she said.

That was it! As I turned it around to see for myself, that was all that *could* have been said, and we both knew it. That year's school picture was the worst of the worst. Red, splotchy, pimply, oily, and gap-toothed. I just stood there, not knowing how to feel.

Suddenly, everything and everybody disappeared from around me. The buildings, sidewalk, light posts, trees, grass, and all the people vanished. I felt like I was on a different planet. There was just me and a voice that was not me that said, *"This is it, Dezlee! If you want to be happy, you can't wait for others; you have to make yourself happy."*

At that moment, all I could do was focus on that voice and the message. The voice felt calm and reassuring, like a parent tenderly leading a child back to their bed after waking up in the night. It felt like a friend was there, and while it started as a voice outside my ears, it moved inside of me. I could feel the words sink into my soul. I knew as clear as a bell that it was coming from God. I felt he would be my friend for life. Even as the girl slipped away, it didn't matter.

Sliding the picture back in the envelope, I slowly walked home. I told myself that day I could either take responsibility for my happiness or let the world determine how I should feel. I decided right then that *I* would be in charge of my happiness. I was not going to wait for anyone or anything! I didn't tell a soul about my encounter that day, not even my mother. It was my experience, and it mattered to me. I didn't want anyone criticizing or changing it. It was much later in life when I finally understood the full impact of that day and how it changed me and the course I took in my life.

That small yet monumental moment lit a spark within me—a tiny light that still flickers whenever I'm called to take responsibility for my own happiness. Life has tested that light many times: when I wasn't invited to a single school dance, when I never had that one best friend, when my husband, Clark, didn't change in the ways I thought he should, and when my children made choices I struggled to accept. Through it all, that light reminded me to keep going—to choose growth over blame, and to keep reaching for the kind of happiness that comes from within.

Happiness Is Our Own Responsibility

Through time, I learned to become my own best friend by knowing and loving myself. I learned with the help of that inner voice from God that I was enough, and I had choices on how to look at life and handle things. I tried hard not to go around blaming other people; instead, I spent my energy on mastering my own emotions and making good decisions.

At the end of the day, I always knew that how I felt was my choice. I didn't want anyone dictating that. Sure, I had plenty of times when I wasn't happy and I desperately wanted to give that responsibility to someone, *anyone*. But each time, I went to that calm, reassuring voice from heaven that essentially said, "You can do this, and I will help." I may not have known a lot of things at that time, but I knew for sure, my happiness was my responsibility.

This very intense, life-changing experience took place when I was young, but it laid a solid pathway in front of me for handling life's challenges. So when I had the unpleasant encounter with my daughter in the bathroom, I was very unhappy, yet very quickly, I didn't blame her for my state of being. It took some tears, a few deep-breathing exercises, and time on the couch, but I knew that *I* needed to take care of my emotions.

With that responsibility at the forefront of my mind that morning, I had a major breakthrough about my approach to happiness. Prior to this, I believed that if I could control people and things around me, then *that* would bring me happiness! Why not? I mean, if everybody did things *my way*, then I would be happy. Haha! I am sure you would be too!

That "logic" had worked for a while when I was young and had only me to worry about. I only had to control myself, and I could do that. But life got complicated and heavy when I applied that same logic to a spouse and four kids, and later a business and employees. It was a hard-earned lesson that happiness is not found in controlling things outside of us, but *inside* of us.

The Master of Your Happiness

And now we are back to ourselves.

Being happy is our responsibility because it is a choice that each one of us makes each and every day. No one else can make that choice for us. We can't be forced into feeling cheerful. We can pretend that we are, and I am certain we have all done that. But that is not the same as feeling it. This is a state of being that starts inside of us . . . *through our conversations with ourselves.*

The first step is to take responsibility for your own happiness. Determine that you are the Master of Your Happiness! Don't give that assignment to someone else. You have to learn how to be happy, regardless of other people or other things. Once you have determined that you are that master, you don't have to wonder where it will come from. Others can add to it, but they cannot be the master.

Happiness is something we all want. Have you met anyone in your life travels whose ultimate goal in life is to be *miserable, depressed, or even sad*? Probably not. Sure, you may know people who can't imagine being happy because they don't know how to be content, positive, or joyful.

I know people who automatically default to thinking things like, *I can't do anything right, I always get stuck in the slowest line, this is going to take forever, it is always me who has to do everything,* and the one that puts a damper on our mindset: *this always happens to me.* It does matter what we say to ourselves, especially when it becomes a habit.

Who and What Are We Choosing To Listen To?

We all have choices, from the thoughts we put in our brains, to the food we put in our mouths, to the things we do with our bodies. These include choices about perspectives, health, jobs, relationships, integrity, beliefs, the words we speak, and much more. Our choices (which start with conversations we have with ourselves), can always revolve around how we take responsibility for our happiness.

Sometimes in life, our choices are limited, but we always have one choice, the most important: our mindset. Mindset is how we think about what is transpiring in any given situation and how it affects us. Dr. Viktor Frankl, a holocaust survivor and author, knew this even in the worst of circumstances, having survived four Nazi German concentration camps. He said, "Everything can be taken from a man but one thing: the last of the human freedoms—to choose one's attitude in any given set of circumstances, to choose one's own way."

If anybody should understand choices under even the most dire and severe circumstances, it would be Dr. Frankl. He chose the conversation he was going to have with himself daily. He called this a "will to meaning"; in other words, giving ourselves meaning to every action, thought, and decision, instead of letting someone else dictate it.

100 Percent Happy?

Now let's pause for a minute. I would like to point out something. It's unrealistic in this wonderful, adventurous, and yet messy life to expect to be merry and bright every minute of every day. It's not going to happen. And that's okay. We are meant to experience all kinds of emotions, and some of those will be the opposite of happiness. It's like knowing and doing everything you can to be healthy, yet knowing you'll still catch an occasional cold. The foundation has been laid, and you know what to do to get back to being healthy.

Lots of people will have every logical ability to make themselves happy, but they'll still put that responsibility onto others. It's like knowing that you need to eat better foods but expecting someone to put the food in front of you. It's like knowing you need to stop being angry, but you continue waiting for other people to stop making you angry! That is just not fair.

Just Who Is Responsible?

Here are a few things to think about when it comes to who holds the responsibility for your happiness.

How do you feel when someone puts their happiness on you—whether it is a friend, your spouse, your mother, a child, your boss? Is it fun? Or does it come with pressure? Can you actually *make* them happy?

This applies to us. Don't require someone to be the caretaker of your happiness.

Here's the beautiful truth: you don't have to stay stuck as someone who doesn't know how to create their own happiness. Relying on others to make you happy will never truly solve the struggle. Happiness is an inside job—it begins with you. But if you're not sure how to do that yet, there's absolutely nothing wrong with asking for help. Reaching out for guidance is a powerful step toward learning how to nurture your own joy.

Which Direction Are You Going?

Happiness is not a place you arrive at in life; it is the direction of your life, a continual path. Talk to anyone who is on that path, and they will say it is taking them to beautiful places! Each of us needs to take responsibility for the direction we are going. Otherwise, we will suffer the consequences. It may not be today, tomorrow, or next year, but eventually it will happen.

If you're not taking on the responsibility, then you have given the steering wheel of your life over to someone else, and if you haven't found out by now, that someone else will eventually disappoint you in some way. They may not even mean to, but human nature says they will.

This is not a bad thing as much as it is a *natural thing*. We are imperfect humans. We do imperfect things! As much as we try, we will at some point fail others and ourselves. It's okay. It's called life and living. However, it is much easier to demand "try again" from ourselves than to demand it from others. This is the reason we need to accept that responsibility for ourselves, get back in the car of our own life, and grab that steering wheel! We are the keepers of our happiness. It needs to be part of our foundation in life, skills that keep us standing and progressing, even when the world wants to knock us down.

Now, believe me, I am not suggesting that we shouldn't let other people around us bring us joy. We certainly should allow room for people to bring goodness and beauty into our lives; this is called living and loving. Connecting our hearts with others will bring light to our souls. However, when "other people" become our *only* source of it, then our light will get dim and we will lose our spark.

Each of us needs other sources, places we can "fill up" our tanks to keep us going on our journey. Connecting to God and ourselves can be those primary sources. After all, who knows better where you want to go, and who you can become?

Happiness is a positive emotion, a good feeling that comes from within us and brings a sense of satisfaction. Aristotle, a Greek philosopher and scientist, describes happiness as "human flourishing." Now that just sounds like a beautiful bouquet, doesn't it? In fact, does anyone ever look at a bouquet of flowers, breathe in their wonderful aroma, and not feel uplifted?

This feeling comes when we make daily choices that help us grow and develop into becoming our best version of ourselves. It sustains us, supports us, and moves us forward. It does not abandon us but produces a feeling of "I am here for you." This kind of long-lasting, foundational happiness is not about what happens to us but what happens inside us.

Author Hank Smith, in his book, *Be Happy,* says this about this subject: "All of this boils down to how we think about our situation and what is happening to us."

Hank tells a story about being a young father when his basement begins flooding. Not just a trickle, which can lead to alarm, but enough to warrant an outright panic! As you can imagine, it was not a happy event. Standing there, with his kids watching his basement fill up with water, Hank knew right then he had a choice about the conversation he was going to have with himself on how to react. His kids were just waiting for Dad to "freak out big time."

He didn't! Instead, Hank gathered his senses, took a deep breath, smiled, and said, "Get your swimsuits on." Now, that's flourishing!

Oh, the memories and fun that followed, simply because of that one Purple CHAT he had with himself, to simply not freak out.

Happiness Is Homemade

Happiness does not come from a package off the shelf, even though the world will tell you that if you buy enough things, you will be happy. That may be the case temporarily, but if we desire long-term homemade happiness deep inside ourselves, it will take work. The work you put into it will be the results you get out of it. Our Creator has already helped us by giving us just what we need, which is our brains, our hearts, and everything else that comes with our beautifully designed body.. But most importantly, we have the ability to choose. It's about who we are inside, not what we have on the outside.

Gandhi, a famous religious and world leader, helps us understand happiness this way, *"Happiness is when what you think, what you say, and what you do are in harmony."*

And so this begs the question: how are we doing on the inside? Do we like ourselves enough to want happiness? Are we thinking, saying, and doing things to align with our greatest happiness?

It's interesting that when I'm speaking to a group or writing it in a book, this is when most people get *completely* uncomfortable because they don't want to ask themselves this question. They may just want to eat a bowl of ice cream instead. It's not easy facing the person in the mirror, especially if you have been avoiding him or her. Yet your happiness is waiting for you. We often think happiness will come to us, when in reality it is waiting for us to choose it.

Why Is Being Responsible for Your Own Happiness Important?

Happiness is a state of being that begins within us—and what happens inside is our responsibility. It grows from connecting with our hearts, where we discover the inner peace and strength that remind us happiness is possible. That peace and strength take root when we are willing to have courageous, honest, and thoughtful conversations with ourselves.

Once we understand that we are responsible for our happiness, we don't have to worry about our happiness being threatened when we have conversations with others. We can then create space for us to extend our hearts to other hearts. Our words and Purple CHATs are a manifestation of our happiness. Make that ultimate choice to be happy and see if your conversations don't begin to change—for the better!

Purple CHAT Questions:

1. Do I choose happiness . . . or do I wait for it?
2. When was the last time I chose to be happy?
3. How could I choose to start my day being happy?

4

The Value Bucket:
Finding You and Your Value

*"Self–worth is so vital to your happiness if
you don't feel good about yourself,
it's hard to feel good about anything else."*
—Sandy Hale

D o you truly know *you*?
Do you trust yourself?
Do you spend time with yourself?
Do you like you?

Maybe your answer is a resounding yes. Maybe not. Either way, that's okay. But if you find yourself unsure or disconnected, I invite you to pause and become curious. There's a version of you worth discovering, knowing, and deeply valuing. And that journey starts with simply being willing to look within. The real you might just be waiting to be found, as expressed in this song by one of my favorite singers, Hilary Weeks (reprinted here with permission given by Hilary Weeks).

I Found Me

*It might seem backwards to some
Like tying your shoes before putting them on
Maybe it is out of sync
Out of order, a mystery
I found YOU then I found me
I had been looking it's true
I just didn't know I was looking for YOU
You introduced me to me
By showing the glimpses of who I could be
I found You then I found me*

It's true. The world is a big place with lots of stuff in it, and we can get lost. Finding ourselves is sort of like the books, *Where's Waldo*, where you are searching for one person in a sea of people and objects. We know we are in there somewhere in the colorful chaos, but where?

This next step is about "Finding You," so you know what kind of Purple CHATs you need to have with yourself. If you have done a good job keeping track of yourself, then I applaud you, and you can just come along for the ride, although you may find some noteworthy insights you haven't considered before. But if you are not sure who You are, or where you are, let's go Find You.

This chapter is about what is happening inside of you, not what you do on the outside. I recognize these two things are very intertwined, and it's easy for confusion to happen. Finding You is about what you think of You, not what you have heard other people say. This is the self-esteem part of our whole selves, and it involves the conversations we have with ourselves.

A lot of people struggle with self-esteem; it is almost an epidemic, as evidenced by the verbal attacks in our society against other people. When we need to attack others verbally (as opposed to a real conversation), it's in direct correlation to something that is going on inside of us that we are ignoring or simply not resolving. We may rationalize otherwise, by saying we are sticking up for what is right or speaking our opinion, but remember, we see the world from the inside out. Something is at the root of the attack from the inside. Our self-esteem is suffering.

We not only attack others with harsh words, but we also do it to ourselves. Sometimes we are not even aware we are doing it. As I suggested earlier with Caroline's story, when we ignore how we talk to ourselves, eventually it can become detrimental.

Pay attention to how you talk to yourself, especially when you are by yourself. Are you saying words that denote your value? Do you take care of yourself physically because you know you are worth it? Does your home and lifestyle reflect that you care about yourself and others around you?

Open your mind to the evidence of how you see and treat yourself. This is important because when you can see yourself better, you can see others better. Then you can have the Purple CHATs you've always wanted to have—those deep, connecting conversations that create incredible relationships.

Revving Up Your Self-Esteem

Try this:

1. **Stand in front of a mirror, alone,** so that you have no distractions or influence from anyone else. You need to be free to be You, which includes permission to be emotional. Hey, why not?

2. **Now look at yourself in the mirror, and I mean LOOK at You.** Most people don't do this because when they do look in the mirror, they are fixing their hair, brushing their teeth, putting on makeup, shaving, or critiquing their choice of clothes for the day. They are *doing*, not truly *looking*. I invite you to stand there, not doing anything.

3. Now, before you can truly see You, I know that you likely need a few minutes to get past what you see on the outside. **Go ahead and look at your hair, makeup, wrinkles, pimples, clothes, tummy, butt, and nose.** Just take it all in.

4. **Now look deeper. Look at the wonder of it all.** How in the world did this body get created? How does it do all the amazing and mysterious stuff it does every day? Your brain, your lungs, and your skin. What a marvel it all is!

5. **When you are ready, take a deep breath** and while exhaling say, **"I like you because you are _____."** (Fill in the blank.) If you need a little help, here is a tiny list to get you started. Add your own wonderful words about yourself.

Honest	Loyal	Kind	Happy
Patient	Spiritual	Creative	Courageous
Forgiving	Grateful	Sensitive	Trustworthy
Thoughtful	Responsible	Outgoing	Compassionate
Practical	Optimistic	Loving	Enthusiastic
Helpful	Organized	Caring	Hardworking

6. **Repeat this at least three times.** I call this "Giving Yourself a Kindness."

This act of giving yourself a kindness may feel uncomfortable at first. Perhaps you've gotten used to only hearing and seeking out what other people think and say about you. You may have a hard time hearing your

HEARTFELT CONNECTIONS

own voice, and when you do hear it, it can sound negative. If you are successful in your first round of looking in the mirror and liking yourself, congratulations! You've just taken a big step toward a better You.

If it turns out to be a huge challenge, it simply means it will take greater courage. This is part of being alive, summoning courage when things get tough. I invite you to try again with a focus of courage and arms flung open to curiosity. Most of us have never been taught to be curious about ourselves, and yet we are all unique! Don't settle. Don't opt out of discovering what's inside yourself. When it seems painful, let yourself get curious. Allow yourself the kindness you would give to others to try when you're ready. Be brave! Be curious! Be the magnificent person you are, and you can succeed.

Your Value Bucket

To help us in front of the mirror, let's talk about our Value Bucket. We all have a Value Bucket, and you will find it may be empty, full, or somewhere in between. Some of us may have never been taught our value and to "hold" our value. Perhaps the bucket has been empty for a long time.

Symbolizing a Value Bucket helps us to visualize a place where we can go to find what we are made of, our qualities, our priorities and values, ethics, desires, and especially our conscious and unconscious beliefs that drive us.

This is what it looks like. Make a fist with one of your hands. Now take that fist and hold it next to your body, either by your heart, or the middle of your chest—wherever it feels the most comfortable. This is where you are going to metaphorically house your bucket.

Make it yours. It's more powerful if you give it a certain style, a certain color, even some vinyl appliqués if you want, with labels like "MY BUCKET" or "HANDLE WITH CARE." How about this one? "WILL ACCEPT TREATS."

In life, one of our greatest adventures is to find and fill our Value Bucket. Our Value Bucket is what makes each one of us, *us*, and we fill it or deplete it by the conversations we have with ourselves. This is no small matter. What is in our Value Bucket determines how we relate to ourselves, to others, and to the world.

Now, to make this more impactful so we can make the changes we want to, let's go deeper than surface-level talk. Look in the mirror and

42

have a courageous, honest, and thoughtful conversation. Consciously decide to place something good about yourself inside your Value Bucket. It doesn't have to be complicated. And I don't want to hear that you can't think of anything. Everybody knows or recognizes something good within themselves. Be truthful with yourself, and your heart will tell you what it is. If it comes easily, that is great! If it is a struggle, you're not alone. Don't hold in your tears if they come. They are there to help you clear your vision. It is time to find positive values to put in your bucket.

To get the most out of the Value Bucket exercise, I have included a very profound way of doing this below. If you are ready for a deeper level of self-discovery, then this is for you, and I encourage you to give it a try. If it's too much to tackle today, no worries. There is always another day. I invite you to remember that feeling guilty or stressed is never helpful, but *stretching* is. This is where you take charge in figuring out the best choices for you and where you are.

Hyrum W. Smith, founder of Franklin Quest, and author of several books, believed that everyone was driven–consciously or unconsciously–by values. In his book, *The 3 Gaps*, and in many of his speaking presentations, he would guide people through an exercise to help them find their governing values. I encourage you to get his book to learn more about governing values. Here is a simplified version of the steps he presents.

From the list below, as well as other values you might think of, circle the top ten that guide you in your life. Keep your initial list to only ten.

Accountability	Achievement	Adaptability	Adventure
Authenticity	Balance	Beauty	Belonging
Caring	Collaboration	Commitment	Community
Compassion	Connection	Cooperation	Courage
Creativity	Curiosity	Dignity	Diversity
Enthusiasm	Excellence	Fairness	Faith
Family	Forgiveness	Fun	Generosity
Grateful	Growth	Happy	Harmony
Honesty	Hope	Humor	Inclusion
Independence	Integrity	Intuition	Joy
Justice	Kindness	Knowledge	Leadership
Legacy	Loving	Loyalty	Openness

Optimism	Patience	Peace	Perseverance
Reliability	Resourcefulness	Respect	Responsibility
Self-Expression	Service	Spirituality	Teamwork
Thoughtful	Tradition	Trustworthy	Truth
Understanding	Vulnerability	Well-being	Wisdom
Write your own:	_____	_____	_____

For the next step, looking only at the ten you've circled, narrow it down from ten to the *three most important values* you hold. Place a star next to your top three only to differentiate them from all others. These undeniably belong in your Value Bucket because they are the ones that govern the way you live your life. Now that you are conscious of them, they can play a special role in your life, and even your Purple CHATs.

For the final step, here's where it gets really interesting. Think of what you would climb a mountain for, cross a parched desert, or a frighteningly tall canyon for, because these values mean *that much* to you. Be ready for your stories to show up about why you chose one value over the other. Now look seriously at each of these three, and decide what order they get to go in:

1. _____   2. _____   3. _____

You are now holding your three most important values in your Bucket, and in order of their importance. Why the order? Because when challenging situations come up–and you know they will–you have vital information about You at your fingertips. Armed with this very powerful knowledge, you can make decisions more easily based on what is important to you. If you have two competing values in any situation, say Integrity and Loyalty, maybe for you Integrity wins out over Loyalty, it just has to. It's who you are. It's how you have unconsciously been choosing to operate, and how you now can consciously operate.

Hyrum Smith says, "The state of harmony between what you value and what you do will lead to inner peace. This can only be achieved when you reach down deep into your core and discover what matters most."

Now pause. Revel in this moment. Look and see Who You Are. You just proved to yourself you have value and there is something not just worth loving, but even liking, about you because of them.

Connecting these two thoughts is key to your Purple CHATs journey: "I have value, therefore I can like myself." And the deeper version is, "I have peace when I live by my values."

This may be a new conversation for some of us to have with ourselves. Imagine saying to yourself, "You are valuable; I like you." If we can have that CHAT and mean it, then it is easier to say exactly the same thing through our words and body language to others. "You are valuable; I like you." Oh, doesn't the world need that! We all need that! Having that courageous, honest, and thoughtful conversation about our amazing value with ourselves, and then with others, could be life-changing.

In this world of "likes" on social media, you need to be able to press the LIKE button for yourself. Don't waste time waiting for others to do it. Fine, if the world does press the LIKE button, but we've got to be okay if they don't. Because if they don't, then what? You *have* to be able to do it.

We are all unique, and it is freeing to validate our uniqueness. "Yes, I am creative. I am loving. Yes, I am loyal." Try it, and others may follow. You have to lead the way to a better You, a better way, and a better life. Press that LIKE button every time! It's like having a high-five, BFF CHAT with yourself. That's right—Best Friends Forever! These courageous, honest, and thoughtful conversations will help you to fill your Value Bucket. Get so good at filling it that you can help others press their own LIKE button too.

Stepping Out of Comfort

We have just participated in some pretty intense deep-dive exercises, and chances are, they may have made you either a bit or extremely uncomfortable.

I have a confession to make: I hate being uncomfortable as much as the next person. But this I do know: comfort keeps you right where you are. There is no movement in comfort, no growth in comfort, and if you want to change your conversations, you have to start by being uncomfortable.

We all long for comfort; it's the relief we need after a long day at work, brings unity when we're with family, and steadies us through difficult seasons. Comfort has its place, and it is a gift we all need.

But when it comes to growth and transformation, comfort isn't what moves us forward. In fact, being comfortable can keep us in uncomfortable situations because they are familiar to us. Change asks more of us. It calls us to stand strong, to step out of what is familiar, and to do the deeper work of becoming who we're meant to be.

And here's the hopeful truth: every step we take outside of comfort is a step towards new possibilities and connections that are waiting for us. Change isn't something to fear; it's the doorway to the life we've been longing for.

This process of recognizing our value and liking ourselves is crucial to loving our whole selves. We become fragmented if we are not able to do this.

You may feel like you're getting along just fine in life without fully accepting or liking yourself. And maybe you are, depending on what *fine* means to you. But ask yourself honestly: is life truly great, or are you settling for less than what you're capable of?

When you discover your core values and begin living by them, you'll realize that life can be far richer, more meaningful, and more fulfilling than you ever imagined.

When you settle, what you are truly doing is just ignoring the gap between your fragmented self and your whole self. This is normal on the human journey at times, but to settle or live that way reveals a lack of self-esteem and self-love. Something will leak out because of that gap, even if you don't recognize it. Emotions like being defensive, negative, offended, judgmental, unhappy, resentful, and hating life, among other things. It shows up as harmful energy and creates great struggles in connecting.

I know it happens to all of us: these unwanted energies show up in conversations that we have every day. We may think it is just how life is. But it doesn't have to be that way. You can be a better you, have better relationships, and experience a much better life.

Honoring your virtues in your Value Bucket helps fill in that gap. The more you honor your values and virtues, the smaller the gap. And the smaller the gap, the more whole you become.

This process doesn't happen overnight or even in a couple of days, but what you will find if you begin to honor them is that they will become a part of your daily routine.

I know I may be going to fantasy land here, but let's just see what happens. What would your day look like if every morning you could push the LIKE button for yourself? Remember this LIKE button is that CHAT you have with you that says, "you have value, you are a good person, and you can do good things." It does not say you are perfect. The LIKE button gives you permission to be more conscious. We can let go of being defensive, critical, judgmental, or irritated. The LIKE button says that when the person on the other end of the phone or in the other car on the highway is rude, you are okay; you don't have to be rude back or honk and scream at them. You are okay, you're good.

Pushing your own LIKE button means being responsible for your conversations. Because here is the thing. You can't tell me that after you have been rude to the person on the phone, or honked the horn and called them a name out loud, that you liked yourself more! In that moment, can you truly say you are being the greatest version of the person you want to be?

It is equally important to like yourself as to love yourself. You deserve to enjoy the time you have on the planet with your number one companion–*you*. You can't get away from yourself, no matter how much ice cream you may eat, no matter how many Netflix series you may binge-watch. You're still there! You go to bed with you every night. You wake up with you every morning. Wouldn't it serve you to *like* the person you see in the mirror?

The beautiful principle here: *Get good with yourself so that you can be good with others, particularly in difficult conversations.*

After you find your top values, know that your life can be far richer and more fulfilling than you ever imagined.

Before we move on, I want to hold up a warning sign: Be aware of Negative Values. As humans, if we are not careful, we can assign too much value to our negative parts. If we do, we let them overtake our positive values. We do this when we refer to ourselves as overweight, not pretty, too short, so shy, a nobody, and not smart. And how about these values that we sometimes come to admire without realizing it: stubbornness, pride, greed, and control. Sound familiar? They do to me, especially the not pretty one. That was a real challenge for me until I figured out how to work on upping a positive value like happiness. I also had a rude awakening when I realized that my wonderful values of strong-willed, independent, take-charge, dominating actions were downright harmful to my marriage relationship. That was a hard one to swallow.

We need to recognize that we *all* have negative values to some degree or another. And part of being good with ourselves is accepting that fact. Accept that we all have good and bad parts about us. The best chance you have for liking yourself is to have your positive traits outweigh the negative. Acknowledge the negative traits, but you don't have to defend them; just accept them.

When I consciously made the decision that I wanted better relationships with my family members, I gave up the need to be right all the time, a trait that I'd fiercely hung onto for way too long. Instead, I worked hard at listening and leading with my heart to connect me more deeply with the ones I love. By doing this, I don't always have things my way, but I have something better, a life full of heartfelt relationships.

It matters how we perceive negative qualities and what we do with them. Sometimes we tend to find something negative about ourselves and hold onto it for dear life as though it is a life preserver. Being right felt to me like that life preserver. If we're not careful, we can attribute too much value to it to the point it even starts to drown out our positive values. Knowing how to handle our values, both positive and negative, is what makes the difference between someone who is at home with themselves and someone who is not. Malcolm Forbes said it this way, "Too many people *over*value what they are not and *under*value what they are.

Why Is Finding You and Pushing the LIKE Button Important to Better Connections?

The better you know yourself and accept yourself, the better you can see and accept others. When we have accepted every part of ourselves, we are better equipped to accept others in all their glory and their messiness. What we practice on ourselves becomes easier during the times we engage with others.

Find You. Love You. Hit that LIKE button!

Purple CHAT Questions:
1. What am I undervaluing about myself?
2. Can I press my own LIKE button?
3. What can I do to replace a negative value or trait with a positive one?

5

Be You!
Living in Peace with Your Conscience

"To be yourself in a world that is constantly
trying to make you something else
is the greatest accomplishment."
—Ralph Waldo Emerson

B elieve it or not, we are still talking about ourselves. It's a big sub-ject. This chapter is about Being You. The reason I have made it so big is because we are the main actors of our lives. No one else can live for us. Nobody can take our place. And how our life flows from us is embedded in our conversations.

It's important to recognize the give-and-take flow of our lives. When we put out energy through living our lives, life flows back to us. This means we can't ignore the significance of ourselves, our words, and our actions. That is not a self-centered statement. If we can believe we are significant, then everyone is significant. What kind of conversations would we have if we internalized that concept?

If that weren't enough, here is another vital thing to internalize: there is no other you anywhere in the world, never has been, and never will be. You are one of a kind, specially made, and heaven-sent. You have purpose, value, and infinite worth. You are worthy of love. You matter! You are needed and you are enough. Isn't that great news!

Here is how someone else I greatly admire said this same thing:

"Today you are you, that is truer than true.
There is no one alive who is you-er than you.
Shout aloud, I am glad to be what I am.
Thank goodness I'm not a ham or a clam,
or a dusty old jar of gooseberry jam.
I am what I am, what a great thing to be.
If I say so myself, happy everyday to me!"
—Dr. Seuss

How I love Dr. Seuss! He makes life simple and puts a smile on your face while doing it. Don't you want to shout from the mountaintop, "I am what I am; what a great thing to be!" after reading that? Wouldn't it be wonderful if we all felt that way about ourselves and could say, "Happy everyday to me!"? How freeing and accepting– and a conversation worth having. If we can say that to ourselves, we probably would be able to say that we are happy that others can be themselves too. Think of the burden that would be lifted in conversations if we could all just be ourselves.

Being yourself can be a hard thing to do, especially when growing up. You may have found, like me, that it actually can be challenging at times as a grown-up! Life is full of comparisons and expectations that can make us question who we are. Then, just when we think we are being ourselves and feel some peace, we often enter a *new* phase of life and have to sort through it again.

It will be different for each one of us. But no matter your age or your circumstance, the BE you part is about you choosing who you are and not letting others choose that for you.

If you are trying to be someone else, then who is going to be you?

Sure, we can learn from other people and even follow their example, but we don't become them. Right now, you can choose to be your own special you. When thinking about your future, let go of expectations. Instead, make a plan to be who you want to be.

Sometimes life challenges sculpt us in negative ways, and we want to go back to who we were before. Acknowledge that if all experiences are for your good, if life happens for you, then you can allow that force, like water sculpting the Grand Canyon, to make a mightier being than before. Trust this. Trust is one of the greatest traits any human can possess, and it leads you to greater significance and peace.

My youngest daughter, Lacey, has experienced some really difficult challenges in her life. By the age of twenty, she admitted to me, "Mom, everyone thinks that I am this happy, outgoing, positive girl, but I'm not. I just act like I am, but it's really not me."

Well, as her mother, I knew that she genuinely once was a naturally outgoing, positive, happy girl, no faking required, but life, as she would say, "pushed all of that out the window."

"You still have it," I told her with all the wisdom and love I had inside. "You just have to go and find it again."

Life can be a roller coaster, marked by downward exhaustion and upward exhilaration. It does and will change us. Sometimes that change is for the good, and sometimes it isn't. Too many of us lose who we once were. Our conversations about ourselves change too.

That's okay, all is not lost. With all the wisdom and love I have for you, may I suggest, "You are still in there somewhere. Make a plan to return to who you truly, genuinely are, or design a different future for you."

Now, if you happen to be someone who hasn't lost who you are, but you want to change an aspect about yourself to be healthier, go for it! Either way, make it *your* choice on who you want to be. Don't let who you are default to life's circumstances or someone else's opinion of you.

One of my favorite things since discovering Purple CHATS has been showing people that I am not in the box they have me in. And quite frankly, I love showing myself that I am not in the box that I think I have put myself in! Despite life's circumstances, learning something new, changing one habit for another, and trying hard things can be very adventurous and rewarding.

And get this: even when you are changing who you are, you are still being you because it is you who is choosing to change!

In my later years, I got a mountain bike. My family and friends were shocked because no one had the idea that I was *that* type of person. I also started watching football and throwing out football jargon. Once again, I was outside of the box that others had put me in. I loved it! It put a smile on my face and helped me enjoy life to a greater capacity. Even writing this book has taken me out of the box I put myself in. Who am I to write a book? Then I thought, *well, why not me!* And then I wrote the book.

The Evolution of Your Self-Belief

Beliefs about ourselves can change over time. As long as I could remember, my conversation with myself was that I was not creative. There it was, that negative value showing up. I told myself very specifically that I could not match colors well or think of designs or arrange things artistically. Now, remember my beautiful older sister who was perfect in every way? Well, it didn't help that she was very creative, and when I compared myself to her, it supported my belief. I had given in to the fact that she was the creative one and I was not. *That's fine,* I thought, settling for less, and I moved on to other things. When I had the opportunity to be creative, I didn't hesitate to pass them by quickly. Every once in a while, I would get brave and attempt to do something creative. When my self-fulfilling prophecy came true and it didn't work out, I would call my sister and cry, "SOS!"

Then, many years later when my husband and I found ourselves in the empty-nester stage, I began to take a couple of chances on being creative. We now had several empty rooms in the house, and I wanted to redecorate them. Just when I started the habit of saying I was not creative and couldn't do it, something finally clicked in me.

I can just as easily say I am creative as to say I'm not creative! I can as easily tell myself I can do this remodel job as I can say I can't.

Here's where it gets interesting: like many times in my journey of these deeper, authentic connections, I experimented. I started saying to myself out loud, "I am creative and can do the remodel job."

Well, shocker . . . but I slowly started to believe it and slowly began to be excited to do it. I knew myself well enough to keep the expectation of the remodel job to a *real* level and not expect it to be perfect. So I proceeded forward with repainting, picking out new bed coverings and pillows, and hanging new paintings on the wall. When I finished, I truly *did* like it! I stood back and was kind of in awe that I'd accomplished what I told myself I could do. It felt good to finally decide to put "Creativity" in my Value Bucket.

Knowing we can hold and value both positive and negative traits, the question we need to ask ourselves is: What qualities in my Value Bucket do I want to keep, and which ones do I want to trade for something else?

Don't let "accepting and embracing every part of us" mean we shouldn't consider making changes. After all, life is about learning and progressing. Maybe you want to add Patience to your bucket or Caring or perhaps tossing out something like Judgmental. Think about it and then make a plan. While we are born with some inherent qualities, you just can't wish that new quality you're striving for into existence. It requires intentional conversations with yourself.

Anger and Anxiety Signal the Need for Change

I remember sitting in a meeting, and the topic being discussed was anger and how to handle it. Not a new subject for most people, as we all experience it to some degree. As the discussion continued, I realized I had some anger in my life, and it affected my conversations. I wanted to change that.

I was married with four kids, and life was pretty demanding, being in the prime of family activities and schedules. I had to make a plan to weed out my anger from my behavior, or it wasn't going to happen. Life was too hectic for wishful thinking. I was determined to have a Purple CHAT with myself to make this change.

I began by recognizing this was my problem and not my husband's, kid's, or anyone else's problem. I was going to take full responsibility for my anger. I figured out my anger showed up when I was frustrated with too much to do and not enough time to get it all done. I had an overloaded schedule of activities and high expectations. This affected my conversations with my kids and also the conversations I was having with myself. I felt like I was constantly yelling, "Hurry up," "Get in the car," "Get out of the car," "Why did you forget that?" and "How many times do I have to tell you?"

It was crazy! And then add family dinner on top of all of that . . . I was not having fun, and neither were the kids. I decided it was time to make a change to my schedule and our family lifestyle. Clark and I, along with the kids, decided to eliminate some activities. It wasn't easy to give up things like piano lessons and some sports activities, but we felt like the result would be worth it.

Whew! It *did* help. But not enough. Those external things changed, but now I needed to work on the internal parts of the problem, which was me.

I committed to myself that when I recognized I was in anger mode, I was going to stop, take a deep breath, and slow myself down. Now, this challenged my core behaviors in two ways. First, I pretty much knew only one speed, which was *fast*. I think fast, I talk fast, I walk fast, I eat fast, and I move fast. For me, this is normal. My life pace did not lean to the "take-your-time mode."

My second behavior was my being adamant about being on time. As long as I can remember, I have always had the mindset that you must arrive at events early or on time; there is no other option. My pet peeve was being late. Even the thought of being late was more than uncomfortable to me. Changing the internal part was not just an adjustment but a new mindset. I was determined to get anger out of my automatic responses.

So I began, and I worked at it and worked at it. It required so much of me mentally. I would repeat the words "slow" and "breathe" in my mind. I would physically make my body switch speeds. And I would convince myself that being late was not the "be-all, end-all" of life. I would do the best I could and then accept my efforts as being good enough. It was hard. It took a lot of concentration, but eventually, over time—lots of time—I got the results I wanted. My conversations were changing, and my relationships were getting better. I felt happier. I had made improvements.

I learned so much from that experience. It opened my mind up to what was possible. I really can control who I am and not let circumstances or people do the controlling. Because here is the thing. If you blame everyone else for your problems, you can change nothing. But if you accept your own responsibility, you can change everything. It's true. And I had changed the conversation I had with myself.

I started another experiment. I wanted to worry less because worrying just made me miserable, and it showed up in my conversations. I identified something I was worrying about and why. If I could do something about it, then I would take action. If I couldn't do anything about it, I decided there was no benefit in worrying. Easier said than done, but because I had enjoyed the success of changing my anger problem, I knew I could accomplish this. It took lots of mental power. I again came up with an action plan and how to carry it out. I changed for the better, much better, and so did my conversations. Do I still have moments of worry? Sure, but now they are moments and not all-consuming brain sappers. It takes effort, time, and determination. But aren't we worth it?

The Process of Becoming

Here's a simple diagram that helps us see what's really going on inside us—the process of becoming who we want to be. It all starts with what's happening in our own head. The way you think shapes how you feel, which influences what you do, and ultimately determines who you become.

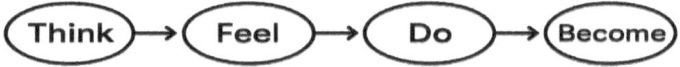

When you look at the chart, try adding the words *positive* or *negative* to see how it plays out. For instance, a **positive thought** leads to **positive feelings**, which inspire **positive actions**, and eventually you **become** someone you feel good about. Of course, the same is true in the other direction—negative thoughts can pull you into a pattern of negative emotions and unhelpful choices, leaving you feeling stuck or frustrated.

You can also flip it around and work backward. Start by asking:

- Who do I want to become?
- What do I need to do to become that person?
- What do I need to feel to take that action?
- What thoughts will help me feel that way?

When you start to see it this way, it's empowering. You realize you're not just reacting to life—you're shaping it. You have far more influence over who you're becoming than you might think. Don't hand that power over to other people or let their opinions steer your story. This is your process. You get to choose how you think, how you feel, what you do, and ultimately, who you become.

I was talking with my friend and her husband one day at their house. I have known this wonderful friend for a very long time. I had seen her struggle through an ugly divorce, have her family ripped apart, and other painful things. She eventually remarried someone who had gone through similar experiences. Our discussion that day was about how they used to go to church but then stopped because of other people. When they did go to church, they were offended by what people would say or not say, and also by the way some people acted towards them.

Yes, it happens. Other people's weaknesses show up in different ways, and so do ours. However, other people's weaknesses should not stop us from being or doing what we want to be or do. Because if we take that stance, it has to work both ways. Would you want your weaknesses to prevent other people from becoming who they want to be?

When you think of your individual situation, you may be saying to yourself, as I once did, "Easier said than done." And I still agree. This is difficult stuff, but not impossible. It takes trying, failing, and trying again.

When my father passed away, I spoke at his funeral. Before I ended, I mentioned something my dad had taught me, "You can accomplish more than you think you can." You see, my dad was raised on a dairy farm in Chinook, Montana. Two unforgettable things about Chinook are summer mosquitoes and bitter cold winters. In those days, you pretty much did what you grew up doing. He thought he was destined to stay on the farm because he didn't think he could do anything else. He married and started a family, and yes, stayed on the farm.

But then something happened.

My father got a vision of who he wanted to become, and it was not a dairy farmer. Not that being a dairy farmer wasn't a worthy occupation, because it was. My grandpa was the best dairy farmer you ever saw! It's just that my dad wanted to become something else. He wanted to experience the idea of "Be You."

He left the farm with his little family, and oh boy, did his parents think he was crazy. Little by little, step by step, with effort and determination, he became who he set out to be. He moved across the country with a family of five kids and received his master's degree in physical education at Indiana University, got a job he loved in Arizona, and excelled at it, earning many awards. At the age of eighty-three, before he passed away, he could not believe all that he had accomplished–warm, happy, and with fewer mosquitoes! I felt his awe that he had done and become much more than he thought he could.

We all can do more and become more than we think we can. We are amazing beings, but change won't happen unless we try.

I have tried and I am still trying and I hope I will forever try, because trying means *learning*. My dad was a huge advocate for education. Going back to college and eventually earning his master's degree transformed him. He quite literally was amazed that he could do that. I am one of those people who decided later in life to go back to college and finish my degree. My dad was my biggest cheerleader. He was more excited about my college experience than I was!

At the time my dad passed away, this book was just a dream. As much as I loved my newfound discoveries of communicating and all the connecting conversations I was having, I didn't truly think I could write a book. But his words kept coming back to me, "You can accomplish more than you think you can." And here I am writing this book.

Here is the thing about learning and trying. Why not?

"Being You" is about showing up as your true self—authentic, genuine, and real. When we do that, our conversations naturally gain those same qualities. It's about embracing all parts of who we are: the strengths and the struggles, the familiar and the new, the polished and the imperfect. Being you isn't about perfection; it's about intention. It's choosing self-acceptance over judgment, and self-awareness over hiding. And when we learn to accept ourselves with compassion, something beautiful happens—it becomes easier to accept others too.

In her book, *Daring Greatly*, Brene Brown writes, "To be authentic, we must cultivate the courage to be imperfect — and vulnerable. We have to believe that we are fundamentally worthy of love and acceptance, just as we are. I've learned that there is no better way to invite more grace, gratitude, and joy into our lives than by mindfully practicing authenticity."

All of this may seem like a lot. The last thing you need to feel is overwhelmed, so here are a few suggestions that may help you: don't take what you don't need; that just creates clutter. Also, take a breath and give yourself some time. Don't do everything at once; try steps, not leaps. Open your mind and you will find what you are looking for.

Why Is Being You Important?

You need to engage in being courageous, honest, and thoughtful with yourself so you can be you. When you have had those conversations with yourself, you will be able to have those same discussions with others and allow them to be who they are.

Purple CHAT Questions:
1. What can I do to be at peace with myself?
2. Am I being my true, authentic self?
3. What am I not accomplishing that I want to accomplish?

— 6 —

Embrace You:
Give Yourself a Hug!

*"I long, as does every human being, to be
at home wherever I find myself."*
–Maya Angelou

One evening, as I was preparing dinner in the kitchen, my daughter Lacey came in. She sat at the counter and started asking me questions for a school assignment. I did my best to answer while chopping, stirring, and, of course, tasting along the way.

After several "what is your favorite" questions she asked, "Who is your best friend?"

My back was turned to her, but without any hesitation, I confidently said, "I am."

"What?" she burst out. "You can't be your own best friend!"

I turned around to see a shocked look on Lacey's face, as if I'd just broken a school rule. This interaction started a great conversation between us, and I hope it starts one inside of you.

This discussion can lead you to some very important questions to ask yourself: What have you embraced in your life? Can you think of a time when you have embraced something or someone with gusto? Was it someone you loved, a soft kitten, a newborn baby, a long-anticipated present, a job change, a spiritual awakening, or maybe a friend's idea about writing a book? Whatever you embraced, I am sure the feelings you experienced were very real and exciting.

When I think about something I truly embrace in my life, it's a bowl of peaches and cream. I know, you might raise an eyebrow and think, "Really?" But the reason I mention peaches and cream is because of the pure joy I feel every time I taste them. I don't have them often, but when peach season rolls around, I'm in heaven. Here's what happens: As soon as I know fresh peaches are in season, I get this feeling of excitement that starts in my stomach, rising to my heart, and preparing my taste buds for pure peach bliss. I eagerly head out to the farmer's market, sometimes even getting a share from generous neighbors with bountiful crops. The smell of peaches fills my kitchen as I unpack the boxes, and especially when I slice into them. Then, when I finally sit down with a bowl of peaches and cream in front of me, I take a bite and can't help but close my eyes and say, "There's nothing better!" In that moment, I savor every bite, soaking in the experience of indulging in my favorite treat. Ooh, I absolutely love that feeling!

Now I know that this may seem a simple, even silly example of embracing something, but the feelings are far from silly. I am being very intentional when I use the word "embrace." Embrace does not simply mean accepting something; it is *how* we do the accepting. Embracing is the mindset that affects how our heart accepts things. That embracing mindset gladly, eagerly, and willingly accepts. Many people may accept a bowl of peaches and cream, but not everyone will embrace it. Many people may accept a newborn kitten into their home, but not everyone will embrace that, either. You see, there is a difference.

When we embrace something, we experience feelings of connection and gratitude. We revel in it! Embracing also helps us to flow *with* something, not against it. This is why it is important to recognize that we cannot control everything. There will be times when giving up control will give you the ability to flow so you can embrace, wholeheartedly.

The question now is: can we do all of this for ourselves?

In other words, can you "Embrace You," all of you, willingly, gladly, and enthusiastically? Every toe, finger, and hair (or absence of hair)? All the good stuff, and not-so-good stuff? The failures and the successes? The real part of life but also the dreams? We all have these categories that show up in our lives, so it helps to know we are all trying to embrace the same things, yet in our own uniquely beautiful way.

Embrace You Physically

Here's a powerful way to get started on embracing yourself. Wrap your arms around yourself and say, "I like you, every bit of you. I'm not perfect, and neither is anybody else."

If you can't do that yet, then try this: take a deep breath, and I mean a really *big*, deep breath. Now exhale, slowly and intentionally. As you do, let all the criticisms, put downs, and judgments leave your mind and body. Let yourself relax and release. Notice how you are feeling as you do this. As your heart calms and your mind clears out all the negative voices, you may find you want to do this exercise several times. This is a kindness you can give to yourself and your nervous system. This is a perfect Purple CHAT to connect body, mind, and spirit.

Now, I know this may seem too simple, and you may think you may need to engage in some other method, yet as you let go of those judgments that keep you from accepting yourself, you will start to find room for embracing yourself. This is a perfect way to connect your body, mind, and spirit.

Remember when I described being in the kitchen with my daughter Lacey and she burst out, "You can't be your own best friend?"

When I turned around to face her and saw that shocked look on her face, I was a little puzzled because I truly believed I *was* my best friend. She, of course, being young and very attached to the "likes" on social media, could not understand how in the world I could say that!

It was the first time that I told Lacey the story of how, as a pimply, red-faced, gap-toothed, lonely girl, I had accepted responsibility for my happiness. "Since then," I explained, "I got to know who I am, I made a plan for being who I wanted to be, and I embraced myself, as me. In the end (well, not the end, because we never stop), I became my own best friend."

Well, Lacey wasn't convinced and started to ask about her dad and friends of mine she knew as being my best friends. "Oh yes, I love your dad and I have friends, as you know, some incredibly *great* friends who have given me priceless friendship. Yet if they were all to go away- and some do because of life circumstances-I still have me. Yes, it took time. I learned to love myself, I learned to trust myself, and I liked being with *me*."

This time, it was Lacey's turn to look puzzled.

"It's all right, Lacey," I said gently. "You have plenty of time to find your own 'Best Friend' inside of you."

If you think the story about me being my own best friend happened overnight, it didn't. It has been a lifetime of journeys that brought good times and bad times, disappointment and fulfillment, heartache and joy. I have gone through and am still experiencing many of life's ups and downs, just like you. I have learned so many beautiful lessons, and continue to do so.

As I connect with people on a deeper level, the more I notice that many people struggle with loving themselves too. We all have voices in our heads that argue against our best selves. But now that I've felt the peace, satisfaction, and joy that comes from always having a best friend, I only hope to help others along the way.

Being a best friend to someone is a common occurrence, but the concept of being your own best friend is not widely considered, let alone accepted. Somehow, we can be a best friend to another by being there for them, supporting them, listening to their sorrows and dreams, and loving them even when it is hard, but we rarely, if ever, do the same for ourselves.

On those days when we desperately need a friend, do we know we have one inside of us? Are we there for ourselves? In the same manner, you can be a best friend to someone else, and embrace yourself as your own best friend. For me, no one knows me better, there's no one whom I trust more, and who is as lovingly honest with me as I am.

There are more lyrics to the song "I Found Me" from Hilary Weeks. Here are the rest, and I appreciate her letting me share these with you because every time I listen to this song, it helps me to embrace ME.

Like the tide being pulled by the moon
Night and day I will follow YOU
Like the puzzle that needs the last piece
You found what's missing and make me complete
I found You, then I found Me
So let's stay together always
You bring out the best in me
I know I'll never be lost again now that
I found You, I found You, I found You, then I found Me

Although the song was written about finding yourself, some people will read it and think about finding a loved one or a best friend, maybe even God. It could be any of those, but let's talk about it being ourselves. Are we treating ourselves like the song suggests? Have you found yourself and embraced yourself, knowing you'll never be lost again? Sometimes it is easier to embrace others and not so easy to do it for ourselves. We deserve to be embraced too!

Embracing involves the heart. Embracing involves connection. Embracing helps us put our lives out there to the world.

There is another important part to embracing ourselves, and that is nurturing ourselves. Besides food and water, which most of us would think about, there are countless ways to nourish ourselves. It's not just about our physical health, but includes our mental, emotional, and spiritual health as well. They all go together; each one affects the other. Besides food and water to stay alive physically, we also need such things as rest, relaxation, love, acceptance, purpose, and hope to be well.

As mentioned previously in this book, some people have never thought about nurturing themselves. They are busy nurturing kids, family members, good friends, coworkers, and sometimes even a stranger. The problem is, as good as it is to do this, it sometimes means we don't get any nourishment for ourselves.

If nurturing is caring for someone so that they can grow, develop, discover, and become, why would we not want to do that for ourselves, especially when we see the benefit in nurturing others?

Nurturing is a form of keeping track of YOU. It is putting effort into the relationship you have with yourself. I can hear it now, the moans and groans and the, "I don't have time."

Hold on. Don't leave the conversation yet.

If you have put all that work into your happiness, of finding and liking yourself, why would you not want to *nurture* yourself? I promise, it doesn't take more time. What it does take is being intentional with the time you already have. This is about you checking in with you, not going overboard; it is about the simple stuff.

Do you need five or even fifteen minutes to yourself?

Do you need to sit on the back porch after dinner before doing the dishes?

Do you need a warm and scented bubble bath?

Do you need to read a book or engage in some meditation instead of watching TV?

How about a walk around the block or simply noticing the brightness of the moon?

I love the way Emily Fonnesbeck in the book, *Whole Fit, Wellness for Life,* talks about nurturing ourselves. She calls it Self-care. "Self-care feels good. It builds a more positive body image, makes us less susceptible to stress and anxiety, improves immunity, increases positive thinking, and leads to patience and compassion for yourself and others. Self-care can feel self-indulgent or selfish to some, but I believe the exact opposite. We are only able to serve others when we have something to give. If we neglect our own needs, we risk deep levels of unhappiness, low self-esteem, resentment, and feeling burned out."

Thank you, Emily! Well said.

Here is what I experienced when I didn't do what Emily said and neglected myself. I will bet money that everyone has a similar story in their lives.

I was married and a mother of four children. Life was hectic with its schedules, activities, ups and downs, and of course, no time for me. Gradually, things started changing for me, and I didn't feel like myself. At first, I thought it was just life and how things were supposed to be when you are a wife, mother, and so many other things. I kept going and doing and trying, often desperately. The more I did, the more numb I became and the less invigorated in life. I had become a robot.

I didn't realize how severe it was until one day my husband, Clark, announced to me that he wanted to start a new exercising and eating program. He asked if I would help and support him in this endeavor. I had never, ever said this before, but I looked at him and replied, "I can't; I have nothing to give."

Clark, not knowing what was going on inside me, was a bit taken aback. I was too. Those words just spilled out. We then proceeded to talk about the situation, and I assured him that I was going to be okay, but I knew I needed to do something. For him, I said I could at least prepare the meals he needed, and then he wanted to know what he could do for me. I was aware enough to know that this was an internal problem inside me, so although his being aware was great, I had to do the work.

Thus began my journey of nurturing me, myself. I did not want to have another conversation where I had to say, "I have nothing to give."

Here's the interesting thing: if you ask the rest of my family members, they won't be able to tell you much about my nurturing journey because to them, everything seemed the same. I still took care of my family and all my other responsibilities; I just was more intentional with the time I had in the day. Nurturing myself did not consume other aspects of my life; I just made different decisions.

Here are some ways that I nurtured myself:

- I started by finding some time to meditate, not a lot of time. Five minutes or more to be still and present and positive. It was simply being aware of me and how I was feeling.
- I slowly made different decisions in my daily habits, such as not watching TV, going to bed earlier instead of staying up late cleaning the house, and getting outside to be active and breathe.

- I began throwing out magazines that just made me want things, listening to better music, reading more, wanting less, and slowing down.
- Then there was my favorite activity: taking a bubble bath, with candles, after the kids went to bed. Even if the dishes weren't done. I did this once a week for a couple of years. If you don't want to fill up a bathtub, grab a cozy blanket and pillow and melt away as you lie in the bathtub pretending you are at a spa!
- In addition, I was more intentional about when to say yes and when to say no. It was a big mindset shift in learning that I am better at handling life when I know that I don't have to do everything that presents itself. I came to realize that saying yes to everything means saying no to the most important things.

Very few people knew what I was going through because I needed to do the nurturing myself. Now, don't get me wrong, we do need other people to nurture us, and that is only natural. However, that can't take the place of us knowing how to nurture ourselves.

After about two years, I felt like myself again, and I must say a better self. It was quite the journey, and I learned so much. I learned that I take much better care of my family and others when I am well-nourished physically, mentally, emotionally, and spiritually.

The story doesn't end there. I continue to give myself drops of nurturing, like watering a plant. I have plants in my house, and frankly, when I neglect them, it shows. When we neglect ourselves by not getting enough nourishment, it shows in the conversations we have and the way we communicate. Nurturing ourselves may feel like just one more thing to do, but as my mother always used to say, "Do the best you can, and angels can do no better."

Why Is Embracing and Nourishing Yourself Important?

When you have embraced yourself, you have found a friend who will be there for you. Everyone needs a friend–a good, trustworthy, reliable friend. By doing this, you will form a foundation that will give you the confidence to handle life and its many conversations. You are in a better position to embrace others.

When you nourish yourself—mind, body, and spirit—you give yourself the strength, clarity, and resilience needed to grow and thrive and find meaningful relationships. It becomes a powerful, positive cycle in helping you find the life you want.

Purple CHAT Questions:

1. How can I "embrace me"?
2. Am I friends with myself?
3. How might others benefit from me nurturing myself?

And Then the Soul:
Finding God in Our Conversations

*"I believe in Christianity as I believe that the
sun has risen: not only because I see it,
but because by it I see everything else."*
—C. S. Lewis

Sometimes in life we feel like everything depends on us—that we have to carry the weight and do all the work alone. I've had those moments or should I say years. But I've come to see there's a bigger picture and better way.

If we truly want heartfelt connections—both with ourselves and with others—we need to begin where the heart began: with God.

When we talk about ourselves, we can't separate the whole of who we are. We are body *and* spirit. We cannot exist without both. Yet because the spirit (or soul, as some call it), is unseen and intangible, it's easy to lose sight of. We often give all our attention to the outer self while leaving the inner self neglected. But to be whole, we must nourish both body and spirit.

And to be honest, my story wouldn't be complete without talking about God. In fact, it feels a little like the old question of the chicken and the egg: did I first discover myself and then find God, or did finding God help me truly discover myself?

This is a dilemma in telling my story. You see, I thought I knew what I was missing and what I was looking for . . . yet I was given miraculous discoveries from Him about deeper love, greater understanding of life, and valuable self-connection that I had no idea I was even missing.

Either way, I will tell you that God was and is an important part of every journey I take, and it started fairly young.

I had no idea in the seventh grade what would become of that young girl who felt like a nobody, who didn't think she would become *any-body*. All I knew as I walked towards home that fateful day was that it was the first time I knew that God cared about me, and that He meant it. It wasn't my dad, mom, brother, or sister who uttered those firm but encouraging words about my own happiness that would change my life from that moment on. I also had no idea the amazing, yet sometimes painstaking, beautiful path that would put me on.

Fast forward to adulthood, parenthood, and survival hood, and life was taking a toll on my spirit. I was trying to do all the right things, and nothing seemed to be going right. I wondered sometimes why I should try so hard.

One evening, I was in my bedroom at the end of a weary day, thinking about my struggles and trying to find some connection with God. Without any thought at all, I flopped my body face-first into the comforter of my bed and was still. I wasn't sure what was happening, but I needed something, anything.

As I lay still, trying to keep from sobbing, that same warm and familiar voice I'd first experienced in my preteens came to me.

"Trust me and I will make your life more beautiful than you thought."

I remained there with my head in my hands and my eyes closed, absorbing that message into my very core.

I knew I had a choice. Suddenly, I raised my head and looked straight in front of me and whispered, "Okay, I will."

With a renewed commitment to stick with God, I forged forward with hope, as He placed amazing people and meaningful experiences on my everyday path, often when I least expected them.

One of those moments happened one day while I was sitting on a gray couch in Jill's really fun, glass-enclosed office. Jill was the director of a real estate sales team. Just a few days earlier, she and John, the team's owner, had offered me a position and I was there to give her my answer.

I was fairly certain I was going to turn it down. Real estate sales just didn't feel like "me." But as I sat down on that couch, something shifted. I couldn't bring myself to say no.

Instead, I opened up to Jill. "I honestly don't know if I want to do this," I admitted. "I don't even know if I can."

She looked me in the eyes and said something I'll never forget:

"We won't let you fail, Dezlee."

There was a pause. I closed my eyes, took a deep breath, and sat in the silence. Then came the answer I didn't expect:

"Okay."

With that single word, I stepped into a whole new world—one filled with growth, deep relationships, and God-inspired connections.

From that day on, Jill and I developed a friendship that far exceeded the boundaries of any glass office. We often found ourselves in heartfelt conversations—conversations that brought tears to our eyes, opened our hearts, and ended with warm, sincere hugs.

Over the next four years, Jill and I had amazing, life-learning, and life-changing connections because of Purple CHATs.

At the end of nearly every chat, Jill would say, "Thank you; you've helped me so much." And I would smile and reply, "No, thank *you*. You've helped me more than you'll ever know."

Here's what I've come to understand: when hearts truly connect, it's never one-sided. In fact, it's rarely even just two-sided. It's a divine triangle—a connection between you, another person, and God. I believe that with God's help, I was able to open my heart to Jill, and she felt that. And in turn, she connected back—not just to me, but to God. And together, we were drawn closer to Him.

That's the life-giving, soul-nourishing power of a Purple CHAT.

Jill's ongoing friendship is a treasured reminder of how God continues to walk beside me. He places people on our paths, not just to support us, but to remind us of His love, His timing, and His plans for us.

I want the same for you.

I hope you find the people, the moments, and the conversations that light up your heart and deepen your relationship with God. Don't overlook the seemingly small encounters—they may be the very things God is using to lead you toward something extraordinary.

I realize that the topic of God and spiritual things can be a sensitive subject in our conversations today. Yet if we go back in history, there were times when societies governed themselves by the word of God, and the Divine was prevalent in everyday conversations. In our "modern age," this has definitely shifted, but all is not lost. I feel it is a sacred privilege and a serious matter to convey how God can be a source to better conversations—and a richer, fuller, more beautiful life.

I believe that everyone's spiritual journey and choices are very *personal*, and so in talking about these things, I hope to edify and uplift only. My greatest desire is to encourage a spiritual journey that will be beneficial to you, your heart, and your relationships.

It begins with our heart, and when you think about it, our hearts began beating through our Creator. He made and knows our hearts. Why would we not go to the One who can help us *connect* our hearts?

Were you aware of the fact that the word "heart" is listed in the Bible more than one thousand times? There is a message in there for us. Truly, think of it: if hearts were united, what a world this would be!

I believe it's important to trust these three things:

1. We are here to learn through our experiences.
2. God knows our hearts.
3. God will help us connect our hearts to others and ourselves.

God is the beginning and the end, with the power to create all things. And as with most things, when something is created, the Creator *loves* that thing He has created. An artist loves her work, a gardener loves his plants, and a parent loves their child. God, who is more capable than any of us to love, loves His creations.

This means you.

If we realized just how much God loves us, we would know that He has the desire to help us. Therefore, I invite you to open your mind to the possibility that you are loved and lovable.

We all need and want to be loved. If you knew that there was Someone from the beginning of time who loves you, wouldn't that matter to you?

Let the idea that you are loved from a greater source (than us humans who struggle with love), fill your soul. *And then be still.* Be courageous, honest, and thoughtful in having this conversation about God with yourself and with Him.

The Journey of the Heart

Some of us may already be on this path of connecting our hearts to God to draw closer to Him and feel His presence in our lives. Others may just be starting to discover that a path even exists. And there may be some who don't yet know where or how to begin. There is no one "right" way to have this deeply personal journey, but I promise you, it is one of the most enriching journeys of your life.

If you're longing to open your heart and experience God's divine love more fully, here are a few simple, powerful ways to begin:

1. Heed Your Conscience: The Whisper of God Within
Every one of us was born with a conscience—that quiet, inner compass

that guides us toward what is good and right. Inherently, we know the difference between right and wrong, yet we override that "knowing." We get busy. Distracted. Numb. Sometimes, we silence that voice, not because we want to, but because the noise of the world drowns it out.

But God speaks through that whisper. To hear it, we must slow down or even stop. We must be willing to tune out the chaos and be present in the stillness.

Your conscience is not just a feeling; it's a divine signal. It takes effort to heed your conscience. It requires awareness, honesty, and humility. You might need to find a quiet space where your soul can breathe, where you can pause long enough to ask: *What am I hearing deep inside?*

That quiet voice guiding you toward compassion, truth, and integrity—that is God within you. Learn to trust it. The more you heed your conscience, the more clearly you will sense His presence. It may be a whole new voice to some of us, but open your heart and mind and discover that connection.

2. Move Toward the Light

Just as the sun warms the earth, nourishes growth, and gives light to our eyes, God's light warms our souls, feeds our spirits, and illuminates our path. But just as we must step into sunlight to feel its warmth, we must also move toward God's light to be changed by it.

Light is and comes from God. He is the source of all light, both physical and spiritual, and He placed that light within each of us when we were created. Even science confirms that all creation radiates light—a reflection of the Creator Himself.

Love is the energy of God's light. When we love, through kind words, gentle actions, and sacrificial care, we release that divine energy into the world. Truth, too, flows from the light of God, reaching our minds, our hearts, and our souls with clarity and purpose. Every spark of love, every moment of truth, every burst of energy that stirs something deep within us, all of it leads us back to the One who is Light itself. Jesus said, *"I am the light of the world. Whoever follows me will never walk in darkness, but will have the light of life,"* (John 8:12).

So move toward the Light. Step closer to God. Let His presence warm your heart, nourish your spirit, and guide your path. His light is not just around you; it lives within you. Make the connection.

3. Use Your Senses to Awaken Your Spirit

God gave us five miraculous senses, not just to survive, but to connect with life and, through it, with Him. But too often we *have* our senses without truly *using* them.

What if we began to *see* the world with more intention? To *feel* with more tenderness? To *listen* with more compassion? What if we used our senses as sacred doorways to encounter God?

- **Look around**: Do you notice the first bloom of spring? The moon in its fullness?
- **Feel:** Have you traced the softness of a rose or held the fragile hand of someone aging?
- **Listen:** Have you truly heard the sound of a lonely soul or the music that lifts your spirit?
- **Taste:** Do you savor the goodness of nourishing food, or even the bitterness that heals?
- **Smell:** Do you breathe in the aroma of fresh bread or the scent of autumn leaves?

4. Choose Gratitude: The Attitude That Opens the Heart

Alongside our senses and conscience, God gave us another sacred gift: the ability to choose our attitude. And gratitude—true, heartfelt gratitude—is one of the most powerful attitudes we can embrace.

It does more than lift your mood; it reshapes your soul. It softens the heart, makes us more receptive to love, more aware of goodness, and more open to God's nearness.

Next time you feel genuinely thankful—even for something small— pause. Feel your heart in that moment. Is it more receptive to love, more aware of goodness, and more open to the presence of God in your life?

That's no accident. A grateful heart creates space for God.

On the other hand, ingratitude hardens the heart. It closes us off. It leaves us feeling distant, disconnected, or stuck. But God is never far and a grateful heart is the doorway back to Him.

If you're seeking to connect more deeply with God, start here: **Give thanks.** Thank Him for breath, for beauty, for moments of peace, or even pain that teaches. Gratitude aligns your spirit with His truth and draws your heart closer to His.

Seeing with Soulsight

When we intentionally nourish our spirits, we become better at what I call *Soulsight*. Like eyesight, it is how and what we see with our souls. They both can see things in very different ways.

Our eyes show us the surface. But our souls? They reveal the depth.

Eyes see trends.	Souls find truth.
Eyes see people.	Souls love hearts.
Eyes see beauty.	Souls create wonder.
Eyes see darkness.	Souls find God.
Eyes see light.	Souls celebrate goodness.

Both kinds of sight are important. But it's Soulsight that leads us into the heart of God.

So, wherever you are on your journey—just beginning, halfway in, or returning after a long detour—know this:

God is closer than you think.
Your heart already knows the way.
And the light you're searching for is already inside you.

Keep walking. Keep seeking. Keep your heart open.

I love the Bible verse that says, "A new heart also will I give you, and a new spirit will I put within you: and I will take away the stony heart out of your flesh, and I will give you a heart of flesh," (Ezekiel 36.26).

In this world today, when so many hearts have turned to stone for one reason or another, who wouldn't want a new heart?

From Reaction to Creation

We need to speak more with our hearts, from our hearts, and to our hearts. It is a quality that makes us human; otherwise, we are just robots, simply reacting to the world around us with little thought. I am sure each of us can say that there are some days when we are living life like a robot. We do schedules, routines, the same jobs, say the same things, and react in the same ways. We move about as though on auto-pilot. We are no longer thinking, and habit becomes the norm.

While routine is not a bad thing in certain aspects of our lives, it is in regard to connecting with others through conversations because auto-pilot wreaks havoc. It causes us to stop listening and understanding each other and even ourselves. I am reminded of another Bible verse that says, "As a man thinketh so is he . . ." (Proverbs 23.7). What are we thinking? Or are we thinking?

To combat the negative consequences of autopilot, we need to find and incorporate our hearts into our daily living and conversations. When we don't do this, we begin to have a hard heart. Having a hard heart is when we stop feeling. We are no longer kind, sympathetic, or loving toward others, and whether we realize it or not, even to ourselves. Arrogance, pride, and rebellion creep in when our hearts are in this hardened state; we are on the downfall, individually and as a society. Having a hard heart is one of the things that alienates us from God and each other– something that should matter to all of us. There is so much brokenness in the world. We see it in relationships, both personal and professional: people hurting people.

If only we realized there is strength in unity. Together, we can achieve so much more than we can on our own. We can heal ourselves, our families, others, and society—if we stop pushing each other away and instead reach out to connect. The goal isn't perfection, but wholeness, and because we're all interconnected, we need one another, including God, to be truly whole.

We all long for this connection, though we're often too guarded to admit it. But God can enhance our perspective of the world around us. Don't turn away because you don't understand, but stay so you can understand. Turning to Him helps us break free from autopilot, enabling us to be fully present and giving us the capacity to deeply connect. Bring God into your everyday life—He is waiting for you.

Why Is Connecting Our Hearts to God Important?

If we want to have more meaningful, heartfelt conversations, we need to start by preparing our own hearts. That begins with aligning our hearts with God. It's hard to remember that even with all our human fumbling and flaws, we are never left to figure it out on our own. Divine help is always available to us to strengthen our relationships, fill our lives with purpose, and bring more joy to our everyday moments. So why not connect into the greatest source of power and love there is?

Purple CHAT Questions:

1. Do I want to connect my heart to God?
2. What am I choosing to focus on?
3. What can I do to experience a change of heart?

Part II: BETTER MESSAGE

Find Your Voice

"In every encounter, we either give life or we drain it. There is no neutral exchange."
—Brennan Maning

— 8 —

And . . . ACTION!
Using Your Voice for Good

"When you find the courage to use your voice, it has the power to positively inspire & change the lives of others."
—Nicole O'Neill

It is now time to take action: to find our voice and use it for good. Look around. The world is hungry for people who are willing to be courageous, honest, and thoughtful with their messages. We, as a society, are very challenged with lies and loneliness, and the way up and out of this, writes author David Brooks, is in connecting our country, and it starts in our communities.

We need to *care* about the place we live in and the relationships we build with those around us. This is how we make the world a better place, one neighbor at a time. Not only do we need each other, we also need a Better Message that connects. Our messages matter, not only for our integrity but for the integrity of society.

We have talked about loving ourselves and connecting with God, so how does that relate to how we love our neighbors? This universal truth asks us to love our neighbor the same way we love ourselves. **So the question is, how are we doing in loving both ourselves and our neighbors?**

Here are some deeper insights into how this truth plays out in everyday life:

1. We love our neighbor, but we don't love ourselves.
2. We love ourselves, but we don't love our neighbor.
3. We don't love ourselves, and we don't love our neighbor.
4. We love ourselves and we love our neighbor.

Everyone fits into one of these categories. As we experience life, we may move from one category to another. Which one do you fit into right now?

You can see from these examples, we can be doing one part of the commandment, but not the other. This God-given commandment is to have a healthy, loving relationship with yourself and then go out and connect in a healthy, loving, and genuinely concerned way with your neighbor.

Who Is My Neighbor?

There are two things to be aware of when we talk about "Love thy neighbor, as thyself," (King James Bible, Matthew 22.39).

The first thing is to be aware of who your neighbor is.

A lot of people will say, "I love my family and friends, and so I am doing just that."

That is terrific, and certainly where we need to start. The bigger picture, however, is realizing your neighbor is all of mankind. What happens when you try to extend love or goodwill to those you don't know? What about the rest of mankind: the cashier at the store who is not moving as fast as you think she should; the city councilman who doesn't think like you; the teacher at school who doesn't try to understand your child; the employer who is grouchy all the time; and the politician who doesn't see the world the way you do.

How do we feel towards each of these neighbors? Because, as you remember, we are taught to love them as ourselves. This means giving them the room to be just as imperfect as we are. The apostle Paul from the Bible says, "Love does no wrong to a neighbor. Love, therefore, is the fulfillment of the law." How profound that is! And sometimes, equally hard.

Don't Fool Yourself

The next thing is to choose not to be fooled by civility. Some people think that because they are civil towards someone, it means they have goodwill towards that person. This is not always true. Being civil is an outward behavior, a *show* of good manners. Genuine goodwill or brotherly love is a feeling from the *heart,* far beyond just good manners.

This happens all the time. Case in point: sometimes we are "civil" to someone in front of their face, but then we turn our backs and roll our eyes or go behind closed doors and verbally tear them apart. We see this in our country today when people take "sides"; some may be civil in person, but then slander that person on social media or in a news broadcast. Now, I am not disowning civility because it is a necessary foundation to a decent society, and I will be the first one in line to advocate for it. Yet civility, as great as it is, is *not the same thing* as loving your neighbor.

It's important not to mistake simple civility for true fulfillment of the commandment—or for the deeper blessings that come when we act from the heart. The effects of missing that deeper connection are easy to see.

For example, in the world today, there are signs of disconnect everywhere. While we can celebrate all the great things happening, we can't turn away from the facts: mental health issues are more rampant, suicides are increasing, and so are mass shootings. These are sure signs of a disconnect. These issues are not easy to discuss, nor to find solutions to. The fact that we are not embracing ourselves or others is, in fact, a major part of the problem.

Loving our neighbors as ourselves does not have to be complicated. It is a matter of embracing, honoring, and valuing our own selves and then sharing that same consideration for others. When we do, it often becomes a win-win situation. I have found in my own life that the more I practice embracing myself, the easier it is to embrace others. I find myself frequently seeking opportunities to embrace people, and the stories of win-win when we have a Better Message.

One of my friends had three teenagers in her home at the same time. As most teens do, they were often upset at one person or another in their world. She felt it was important to listen to their grumblings and make sure they felt heard and understood. However, as she was contemplating how often the conversations would revolve around personal attacks, she realized she needed to have a better message to help them and her turn things around.

Then one day, for a family activity, she had her kids bake chocolate chip cookies with her. She told them that after baking them, they were going to deliver them. The kids got incredibly excited and created plates of these special, mouthwatering treats, making them look beautiful and wrapping them carefully.

That's when the mom announced that each of them, including her, was going to deliver these plates of cookies to the specific person they were having the hardest time with at that moment. Well, you can imagine the looks they gave her and the grumpy noises being cranky as they piled into the minivan, and then the awkward silence as they drove towards their destinations.

But lo and behold, an hour later, all four were happily chattering on their way home, laughing about the surprised faces that greeted them at their "arch-enemies" homes. There were hugs exchanged, walls that came down, and small miracles all made possible by a plate of chocolate chip cookies.

They "got" Mom's Better Message.

Our fullest life is led when we can love ourselves and then love others. We want to be in a position to handle life so we can help other people.

Why Is *Love Thy Neighbor as Thyself* Important?

This divine principle is the entire reason for Purple CHATs. To love yourself and your neighbor. By doing that, we will connect with God, ourselves, and others. It will lead us to the relationships and purpose-filled life we all seek.

Purple CHAT Questions:

1. How could I choose to be more loving to my neighbor?
2. Would loving myself make a difference in how I show up for others?
3. Can I do both?

9

Feed Your Brain:
Deciding What Is Important
& What Is Not

*"Achieving a more conscious participation in a
richer story proves a great gift after all."*
—James Hollis

D id you know there is a scientific way to achieve better conversations? It all starts with the brain. As wonderful as that evidence
can be, which we'll discuss, the problem is that when we think of conversations, we typically *don't* check out our brain first to see what kind
of state it is in. We just think about what we want to say! The issue is
that if our brain is not functioning well at the moment, then our conversations are not going to go well, either.

I was driving home from work one day, and I had the conversation
all planned out in my mind. I was going to use "these" words, with
"this" tone, *and I am going to mean it this time!* The timing had to
be just right because it was about money, again, and, as it turns out,
this is generally the toughest conversation to have between spouses,
especially in my marriage.

All the way home, I was getting into prepared mode. I parked in the
garage, but upon entering the house, I suddenly realized I was fam-
ished. For some reason, the thought that *I'm starving* took over my
conversation focus.

My husband, Clark, was downstairs in his office, so I decided to find
something quick to eat. It wasn't too quick; I permitted myself to eat
some real food, not just snacks. Once I was finished eating, it was time
to get back to the conversation.

Conversation? What is the big deal about having that conversation?

All of a sudden, my brain had switched gears. The conversation
did not look as big or daunting as it had previously. The more I
thought about having the money conversation, the more I realized
I never really needed to have it in the first place! For some reason,

there wasn't the dire need for this difficult conversation that I had planned in my head.

What just happened? Why was I feeling so different about the conversation now? After some pondering on the situation, I discovered that it all changed when *I* pulled myself out of starving mode by nourishing myself.

The funny thing is, scientists can tell us exactly what happened. It's not that complicated. They say it's just a hungry brain. You've heard the term "hangry." Well, it's a real thing! The brain is the CEO or the boss of us, and it needs nourishment to operate satisfactorily. Feed the brain good stuff, and it will do its job. But if not, watch out! It will get "hangry" and give you fits of misinformation!

Research shows that when the brain is lacking proper nutrition, there is a change in our mental functioning *before* there is a physical change. [2]This change in mental functioning could include changes in mood, like irritability and overall grumpiness. Thus, in my story, my brain was freaking out a little because I was starving, and it started to exaggerate things, creating whirling thoughts that stirred emotions of anger and others. Yet once I was nice to it and fed it, my brain decided to return to normal. *Thank you, brain!* You just saved me from making a conversation much bigger than it needed to be.

This Isn't About Shoving Thoughts or Feelings Down

Now, I am not saying you should eat something in place of having a difficult conversation. No, not at all. Doing that will only hand us more proven problems like eating disorders and diseases when we don't own our voices and our truths. What I am saying is you should be *aware* of yourself and what kind of state you are in before initiating any serious conversation. Nutrition and hydration powerfully affect our mental state, which affects the words we choose, which affects the outcome of our conversations.

Logically, then, knowing this information, if you want better conversations, choose better words, which require optimal brain function. Pay attention to yourself and see if it's not true. If you are feeling upset,

---

[2] https://www.health.harvard.edu/blog/nutritional-psychiatry-your-brain-on-food-201511168 626. September 18,2022; https://www.uclahealth.org/news/article/you-are-what-you-eat-diet-may-affect-your-mood-and-brain October 23, 2023

angry, tense, or other negative feelings, before you go say something to someone that you may regret, stop and ask yourself if you might need to feed your brain. It is great preventive medicine as opposed to feeling regret for something said. Since then, I have experienced this phenomenon enough to know that if my brain gets all worked up over something, I better quickly think about nourishing myself before I engage in anything important.

Growing up (and even now), my mother's solution to most things was food. In our family, she is famous for saying, "Here, have something to eat," and then she starts dishing out food! Now you may think that is funny, but everyone loves my mother, not for the food, but because they always felt better being around her. One of my sisters laughingly labeled it: "Eating Your Feelings." Yet Mom wasn't too far off. As a nurse, although she never explained her reasoning for constantly feeding people, she understood that we, our brains, and our emotions work better when they are sufficiently nourished. Eating, of course, does not mean this is the solution to making problems go away. (Oh, if only it did!) It means it is the solution to *how* we think about and solve our problems with our brains. Being nourished is one way to help us think about the right message–a better message.

Mindfulness: Nutrition, Rest, and Serenity

I can't tell you the difference this one discovery has made in my conversations, especially the challenging ones that take a lot of brain power. I've learned this not only applies to getting food to the brain, but also being aware of our whole body. Consider this: being tired physically or being emotionally drained is not the best way to enter into difficult conversations, either. I have often wondered why we as a species often want to hash things out with our spouse or kids at the *end* of the day, when we are all worn down from life! Can you see why taking care of yourself first is the way to better your communications? It is exactly like the oxygen mask on an airplane. Put it on you first, so that you will be in a better position to assist others with their oxygen masks.

Different Types of Conversations

This knowledge about rest, nourishment, and timing helps us to recognize that there are different types of conversations that require different levels of energy and self-mastery.

- There are surface or courtesy conversations. These are your meet and greet ones. Nice, but has no depth.
- There are fun-loving conversations, ones that are positive and done with laughter.
- There are problem-solving conversations that require focus and brain power.
- There are intimate, loving conversations where the heart takes the lead.
- There are heart-to-heart conversations with someone who needs more listening than talking.

And then the one that we all dread, that is, until you learn about Purple CHATs:

- There are difficult, hard, and sometimes excruciating conversations that require everything and more from you.

Have you ever had someone come up to you and start a conversation, and afterwards you thought, *Boy, they sure could have handled that differently* or *That wasn't the problem* or *What in the heck were they talking about?*

In those cases, a better message would have benefited both of you. With a little more thought, our messages can be more meaningful. It just takes the habit of thinking before we speak, instead of speaking before we think.

In the beginning, this may feel exhausting because we tell ourselves it is just one more thing to do. But here is the truth: you can choose to believe that one and shy away from the best conversations of your life. **Or,** you can put this on your to-do list and take something off, like being too busy, too controlling, or too negative. You decide.

The other truth is powerful: that once you practice and learn how to create better messages, stronger, better communication will come naturally, and you won't have to have it on your to-do list.

Four Steps to Consciously Create Better Messages

So let's talk about what things matter when you want a better message. This is not to take away your everyday spontaneous interactions—although let's get real; if those casual impulsive conversations are causing grief for you and your loved ones, then maybe it is for those too. But this information is precisely for the *conversations that matter* and where you want to find more connection and understanding.

1. First, make sure your brain is fed, and you are aware of the state of your body.
2. Determine just what time of the day would be most beneficial to have this conversation.
3. Does it need attention now, or can it wait?
   a. Sometimes a conversation is urgent and necessary right away in terms of medical, financial, emotional, or physical crises–they simply cannot be pushed off.
   b. Oftentimes, a conversation feels urgent because of that malnourished brain stirring up emotions. Give yourself time, space, energy, and nourishment to be clear about it, if possible.
4. Am I good with myself, and have I checked my *attitude*?

I will assure you that if you think about these four things first, your conversations will change for the better. Eventually, checking in with yourself will become very natural to you.

These four steps will help you decide what is an important conversation and what is not a conversation at all. Pick two important conversations this week, and try this as an experiment. See what happens!

I learned to apply these steps in my conversations with my kids when they arrived home from school. They would come through the door and throw their stuff down right in the middle of the room, where, of course, I didn't want them to! Daily, it used to be a big fight, but then I decided to try a different way. I intentionally made sure my brain was working well and that I was aware of my body. I decided that right at the moment they came through the door—after a long day at school, where they had to listen to instructions all day—was not the time to talk about where their stuff landed! In all reality, it could wait until after I asked them about their day, they had a snack to feed their brains and they felt loved. By this point, it wasn't about me and what I wanted, but it was about making a connection. In the end, there didn't need to be a fight about the stuff on the floor; there was a real caring conversation, after which they picked their stuff up without moaning and groaning because their needs were met as kids. When I had successes like this one, it became easier and easier to sort out what mattered most and what didn't.

Not Avoiding: Planning Quality Outcomes

I don't want you to think that this is about avoiding conversations because it's not. It's about the *quality* of our conversations. That quality includes thought, words, timing, and presentation. It's not just about short-term gains, which can feel important, but are shallow. Instead, these are about long-term gains in your most valued long-term relationships. In my example above, I didn't avoid having the discussion about picking up the stuff on the floor; I just had it in a more connected way instead of a confrontational way. Relationships flow more easily when you choose to participate more intentionally.

Why Is Being Mindful Important to Effective Conversations?

We have a responsibility with our words. It should be embedded in our integrity. I invite you to slow down and choose not to be sloppy with your messages. Mindfulness gives us the pause we need to think before speaking and ask: *Is this the right time? Am I in the right state of mind? What truly matters here?* By checking in with ourselves first, we create space for more meaningful, respectful, and productive conversations that build rather than hurt relationships.

Purple CHAT Questions:

1. Do I neglect my brain power?
2. Do I speak before I take time to think?
3. Would nourishing myself really make a difference in my emotions?

10

Put Your Glasses On:
Being Aware of My Relationships

*"Seeing the bigger picture opens your
eyes to what is the truth."*
—Wadada Leo Smith

Yes, it happened to me.

I didn't want it to. I tried to prevent it, but somehow my eyesight was changing–deteriorating, to be exact.

My vision challenge first began with small print. (It would help if we could get small print banned from the earth! Come on, people, at least make it readable.)

Trying not to give in to the fact that old age signs were appearing, I just started holding things at different distances from my eyes. The prescription bottle, food labels, and magazines were getting farther and farther away from me. Oh, I fought it. I was not about to give in. I worked hard at holding things at the "right" distance. I squinted, then I didn't, then I squinted again, in hopes of readjusting my eyes. I would even nonchalantly ask my kids to read things for me in the store or at home in the kitchen. "Hey, read this label for me while I sort through the bananas, will you?" I thought for sure I could beat this thing!

Then, one day, I sat down on the couch to do one of my favorite things: read a book, and I couldn't. I couldn't do it unless I held the book up and away from me.

Dang it! I had arrived!

Finally, I thought, *enough is enough,* and I stopped fighting it. I went to the store and bought reader glasses.

Wow! Did that change my world! *Why did it take me so long to do this?* I could see. Life was before my eyes again.

When You Change the Way You Look at Things, the Things You Look at Change

Things change, with or without our consent. Change happens naturally with living things such as plants, animals, and people because they are made to change. Nature has been in control long before we came along. Families and relationships change because they are made up of people who change . . . *by nature.*

However, it's not just change that we have to come to grips with, but the more important question of what do we do when things change? Do we ignore change and cross our fingers that our eyesight really isn't going to change? Do we fight against change no matter what? Do we find a band-aid solution? Or do we accept that a change is happening and put our energy into the best way to handle change?

Change *can* be a good thing, even great, if we let it. Sometimes we react, going into fight mode, simply because we are facing change and we don't stop to think about what is happening . . . and avoid getting those darn reader glasses!

After I finally settled into the change with my eyes, I experienced a "seeing moment." Usually, when I was at home, I did not wear my glasses unless I was reading or in front of the computer. That meant when I was doing regular chores around the house, I didn't need to wear my glasses. Well, I was in for a shock!

I walked into my bathroom one day with my glasses on because I had just been reading. While standing at my bathroom sink, I was startled at what I saw through my glasses. My bathroom was not at all as clean as I thought it was. With my glasses on, I could suddenly see stuff that I could not see with my glasses off!

Ooh, I am sure you don't want details on bathroom hair and makeup and whatever else, so I will spare you, but let me assure you . . . *it was there.* Now, the reason I was so shocked is that I am a very conscious bathroom cleaner! Yup, imagine me, spray bottles in my tool belt. You see, I clean regularly. *I don't have dirty bathroom issues!*

And yet, I stood there with my glasses and looked at the stuff that had accumulated on the bathroom counter and floors. Then I took my glasses off, and amazingly, the stuff disappeared! Ha! Are you with me here?

Oh my gosh! Here I thought my bathroom appeared one way when it was really another way. It took me a minute to come to terms with this. It wasn't so much that my bathroom was dirtier than I thought, but it was the fact that the bathroom was really *in a different condition* than what I thought it was.

The fact of the matter was that I was not seeing the bathroom very clearly. Yes, I know, we are only talking about a bathroom here, but it was the principle of the thing that bugged me! What else was I not seeing clearly?

I went downstairs to my kitchen, and yep, there was stuff there that I saw with my glasses on. Now, don't get me wrong, I didn't walk around half blind or anything. I could see just fine, except when it came to the smallish stuff, which may or may not be a big deal. I mean, a bit of hair on the bathroom counter and some crumbs in the corners of the kitchen are not earth-shattering. But what could be, at least earth-shifting, was thinking that stuff didn't exist when it really did. I had to have a moment to come to grips with the fact that I was not seeing the true, full picture.

After that little experience of seeing more clearly with my glasses on, I began to think about what else I might not be seeing clearly.

Am I not seeing my relationship with my spouse and kids as clearly as I could be?

How about my relationship with my coworkers or with clients?

What is my attitude about other drivers on the road or people in line ahead of me?

Do I act as though life owes me something?

Do I think I am a good listener when I'm not?

Do I have control of my body language, or am I missing something?

I had to realize that each of us can only see what we see. But maybe we need to find a different way to see sometimes. Maybe we don't always have to walk into the bathroom with our glasses on, but maybe we should do it more often than we have been. Maybe we should try more often to look at our relationships with better glasses.

Once I saw the true state of my bathroom and kitchen, I was able to make a choice. I decided to clean with my glasses on. That's all—no big announcement to the world or change in my schedule. I just made a little change to put my glasses on.

Choosing to "Wear Glasses" in Your Relationships

What little change can you make so you can see things about your conversations and relationships more clearly? Don't just use your eyes, but feel with your *heart*. Maybe it's being a better listener, changing your tone, choosing different words, or slowing down to be present. Little things can make a big difference.

So, how do we go about seeing intangible things like conversations, relations, intent, expectations, thoughts, and emotions? Do we think we know what these look like? Do we assume we are doing a good job in these areas? After my eye-opening bathroom experience, I decided to see what would happen if I asked some people in my life this question:

"Hey, I genuinely care about our relationship. Is there something I am not seeing or doing that would make our relationship better?"

Wow! Some amazing lessons for me personally rose to the surface.

I started by asking my husband, Clark, about our relationship. I was genuine when I spoke to him and repeated: "Hey, I really care about our relationship. Is there something I am not seeing or doing that would make our relationship better?"

I already knew crumbs were lying around in corners. My problem was figuring out how to clean them up. I further asked him this question: "What am I not understanding when we discuss finances?" You see, we have been married for thirty-five years, and I am sorry, folks, but this discussion has been—and still is—messy. (I know; if you can't understand that, bless you, and if you do understand it, then here is a hug.)

In the past, it was always messy, and we always left the discussion before we got the mess cleaned up. Well, this time, I was determined to start cleaning up the mess. I wasn't going to take my glasses off and have them disappear. I was honest in admitting that there was a problem, and I put on my courageous cleaning gloves. I thought about what words to use so that we could keep our weapons of war at bay.

At first, he didn't want to say anything, not wanting to get into the whole "not going well" conversation. But I knew the critical part of being courageous was being vulnerable. I had to be the first to embrace being vulnerable. I admitted to him, "I know I have not been communicating well when it comes to our finances. I need your help in knowing how to change that."

As soon as I admitted to being at least part of the problem and wanting to change that, Clark's face changed. He began to think maybe he really could say something. Slowly, ever so slowly and carefully, he began to tell me that my selection of certain words in our finance discussions were just not working for him.

When I heard that, it was really hard to continue. I already knew there was a problem, but I was surprised at what the problem was. I took a long, deep breath. Being more concerned about the message than being right, I harnessed my emotions and thoughts and moved forward on discovering what those words were that didn't sit well with him .

The particular words or phrases were not the important discovery I made that day. What I did discover was that certain words *meant and felt different to him than to me*. I had no idea! I had been assuming that all words meant and felt the same to both of us. For example, when I said "It's crunch time," to me that meant it's time to implement an action plan. To Clark, however, "crunch time" meant failure, and that nothing he had done in the past mattered.

Another one was when I said, "Can we talk about our finances?" To me, that meant we needed to touch base and make sure we were on the same page. To him, it meant that I thought he didn't know what was going on with our finances.

I was floored. How could this be! I speak, you understand. *Isn't that how it works?*

This continued to be a difficult conversation. It was mentally and physically demanding. But the discoveries that happened that day were priceless. That interaction changed us. It changed our conversations, which enhanced our relationship, and it changed our perception of our finances. We were courageous enough to do the hard work, honest enough to admit there was a problem, and thoughtful enough to keep our words and emotions in check. Exhausting? Yes! Worth the understanding gained and progress made? Absolutely!

You can ask these types of questions in so many different ways, depending on the relationship and situation. Make sure you ask these questions only if you are in a place to really hear what they have to say, and if you really want to see what you're not seeing. This requires that internal, conscious nourishment we discussed, so you will not be defensive about something they might say. Instead, you sincerely want to understand how the relationship is going. Let go of the judgment about what the other person may say and come with a desire to learn.

A Vital Caveat to This Question

These questions can bring about an awkward conversation if you're not careful. They are a perfect example of a courageous, honest, and thoughtful Purple CHAT.

- **Courageous** because you want to do the hard work to improve the relationship instead of ignoring what you can't see.
- **Honest** because you know the question needs to be asked in some form or another. You want to see what you're not seeing.
- **Thoughtful** because you are going to think about the right words to use, and then how to handle yourself when the conversation actually takes place.

It will be great! Lots of good stuff will happen in your relationships, and your life will change. That's not to say it will be easy. You could encounter negative feedback and maybe even some pain, but be brave and know that the clouds will part to show a clearer path that will lead you to better relationships.

Glasses or no glasses, we need to be aware that things may not be as we see them. If we look harder and care more deeply, would we be willing to have courageous, honest, and thoughtful conversations to clean up the messes?

Here are some suggestions:

1. Be aware that there may be some crumbs you are not seeing.
2. Have the desire to clean up the messes.
3. Be open: ask to understand, not to be right.
4. Be courageous, honest, and thoughtful.
5. And be HAPPY!

Why Is Putting Your Glasses on Important?

Seeing things as they truly are helps when it comes to having deeply meaningful and transformative conversations. It creates more understanding AND being understood. You can't change or fix what you don't know about or don't understand, but these conversations open doors to significantly richer, authentic relationships. I promise, it's that rewarding!

Purple CHAT Questions:

1. Am I seeing things clearly?
2. Could I benefit from putting glasses on?
3. Who should I ask, "Is there something I'm not seeing?"

— 11—
Wait a Minute!
Whose Mess Is This?

"We are dangerous when we are not conscious
of our responsibility for how we behave, think, and feel."
—Marshall B. Rosenberg

In our family, we often car-swapped when we had kids at home who could drive. Someone would need a certain vehicle to take to school, a sporting event, or other trip, so we played musical cars.

One particular time, this involved my husband, Clark, one of my daughters, and me. I gave up the car I usually drive and ended up with another family car. Note that the car I gave up was clean and had more than half a tank of gas. The car I received in return, however, was dirty and had less than half a tank of gas. "It always happens this way," I muttered to myself as the other two had already driven away. "I always get the short end of the deal." I was not a happy camper.

Once I calmed down and looked at the situation, I decided to take some of my own medicine and have a courageous, honest, and thoughtful conversation when we were all together again.

I started formulating my message, and boy, was it going to be a good one! I started thinking about every time we swapped cars. I thought about how they were never being considerate when we had to trade cars, and on and on. I was getting a pretty good message together and the delivery!

Then this thought came to me, "Whose mess is this anyway? Could this be *my* mess?" All of a sudden, I realized that over all the years of swapping cars, we'd never had the conversation about what needs to happen when we swap cars! Not ever. I never brought up my desire to have the car clean and full of gas when another person was going to drive it. I kept hoping that they would eventually think like I did; wasn't that what they were supposed to do?

That's when I realized that my being upset about the situation was my problem and not theirs. I needed to take care of my emotions and not put them on my family members. This was taking personal responsibility for my own emotions and experiences. Next, I needed to change my message to a better one, switching it from an accusing one to one of understanding. **Here's the clincher: I needed to talk about my expectations before I could expect the expectations!** The principle here is don't just think about expectations, express them, and the why behind them. The fact was, we needed to talk about how the car swapping needed to work for everybody.

This whole mess ended up not being a mess at all once *I* sorted it out. Those conversations with ourselves are so important. I calmed my emotions down and decided not to accuse them of anything. Next time we had to swap cars, I simply stated that I would like to get a car that was clean and full of gas. "Is that possible?" I asked aloud. Lo and behold, somehow it wasn't a big deal to anyone else! Who knew because we had never had that discussion before! They agreed to the car swapping rules, and everyone went away happy. Next time we did musical cars, everyone remembered, and I was ecstatic to find a clean car with an almost full tank of gas. Whew! It did matter what kind of conversation I had with them.

It's easy to see why we hesitate or avoid difficult conversations. But what if the real issue isn't the conversation itself—it's our lack of clarity? Have we really thought about *what* we want to say and *who* we need to say it to? Or do we rush in, focused only on ourselves and what we want, and end up creating the very mess we hoped to avoid?

Let's be realistic. It's impossible to navigate life and relationships without encountering messes. This is because:

> Families are messy.
> Relationships are messy.
> We are messy.
> Houses are messy.
> Work is messy.
> Traffic is messy.
> Garages are messy.

These and other things in our lives are messy because they have a certain level of confusion, difficulty, and disarray associated with them. It's how life is, chaotic and adventurous, fun and exhausting, beautiful and messy.

So, what do we do with messes? We certainly can avoid them by engaging very little in life. On the other hand, we can add to them by living life carelessly. But there is still another option.

The best way to tackle messes that seem overwhelming is to figure things out, sift through it so you can get some clarity. Just like the car-swapping story, I could have thought the mess was Clark's and my daughter's fault and gone in and accused them of things that I didn't like. Heaven knew it had happened before. Or I could have taken responsibility for my own emotions and changed the conversation to one of *solving a problem collectively, not just my way.*

Conversations are how we have relationships with family, friends, and anyone else that comes into our world. Relationships are messy, they just are. I am not saying that every time we open our mouths we need to have a well-planned message coming out, but to have courageous, honest, and thoughtful conversations, we do. Are we having enough of those? Are we adding to the mess or straightening out the problems we encounter in relationships? To have the right message involves figuring out whose mess it is. Is it something that we need to take care of ourselves, or does it involve someone else, and who is that person?

There is more than one way to have a conversation, but when we are only thinking of ourselves, well then, we are only thinking of one way! That is why being good with yourself and taking care of yourself *does* matter when it comes to the message you are going to deliver. When you have taken care of yourself, then you have freed up space and energy to think of the other person when delivering your message–and listening to theirs.

More than ever, our messages need a little more thought to them . . . with a little more heart. I have heard it said that people are too sensitive, that you can't say anything without offending someone. And yes, while that is happening, this is also true: as a society, we have become too INsensitive in the way we speak. Our language, and even our thinking has become sloppy and lazy. Part of the problem is that no one is requiring us to put our best foot forward. Technology has made conversations fast, easy, and let's not forget, faceless too. Life is fast-paced, stressful, competitive, and more demanding than ever, and all of that shows up in how we talk to each other. What a mess!

Do any of these sound familiar?

- We are mad at our spouse for coming home late from work, but in reality, we just had a bad day.
- Our coworker is annoying, but in reality, we are struggling to meet a deadline.
- We yell at the kids to pick up their school stuff, but in reality we are tired and have not taken care of ourselves.
- Our boss is so demanding, but in reality we are having personal problems at home.
- Maybe we tell ourselves that life sucks, but in reality we are just comparing ourselves to what we see on social media.

Can you see how easy it is to think it is a certain problem? If we really think about what is going on, we could discover the real problem, and have more of a courageous, honest, and thoughtful conversation. This requires pausing and some self-reflection.

- Instead of jumping all over our spouses for being late, maybe we could ask how their day went. We just might find out they had a bad day too, and then the conversation could be about how to help and support each other instead of the game of blame and defend.
- Instead of confronting our coworker about how annoying he is, perhaps we could talk to him in an effort to get to know him.
- Instead of yelling at the kids, tell them we need help because we overdid and are tired.
- Instead of being negative about the boss, realize he has a job to do too, and choose to have an honest conversation on what you *both* need, not just you.
- And, instead of telling yourself that life sucks, start to list the reasons that life is good.

Can you see that it does make a difference when you choose the right message? Sometimes the mess is yours and yours only. Sometimes the mess is theirs, and sometimes it is both of yours. Just take some time to figure that out because it does matter. Having a Purple CHAT requires you to be honest about whose mess it is and then, in a thoughtful way, be courageous enough to have that conversation that you need to have.

Here is one way to think of whose mess it is. If you decide that this is your mess, then you can't go into the conversation blaming others. You need to take responsibility and ask for help if you need it. If the mess is someone else's, you go into the conversation asking to understand and offering help. If the mess is both of yours, then you go into the conversation working together to find a solution.

Messy situations are not always about facts, so be careful when dealing with opinions. An opinion belongs to the person who expresses it—it's not someone else's responsibility. Whatever you do, try not to turn your opinion into someone else's mess. Also, be careful not to turn opinions into facts.

Messy situations aren't always about facts, so be careful when dealing with opinions. An opinion belongs to the person who expresses it—it's not someone else's responsibility. Whatever you do, try not to turn your opinion into someone else's mess. And just as important, don't mistake opinions for facts.

A classic example of this is when people start talking about politics. Need I say more? I have several family members with whom it is hard to have a two-way discussion. The emotions are highly charged because everybody wants the other person to see it from their viewpoint. It's hard to accept the fact that your spouse, sister, or son may not think like you. For some reason, we feel threatened by other people's feelings. Instead, we should be curious about others' opinions and ask why they feel a certain way instead of making belittling comments. Learning is always better than defending. This is much easier to do when we go back to being at home with ourselves and our opinions. If you don't like being attacked for your opinion, then don't attack others for theirs. It's often said, "He who asks the questions learns the most." Don't miss out on learning something that could lead to connecting while also avoiding a mess.

Remember, if you want to have opinions, then be considerate of other people having opinions as well. This goes back to, "Love thy neighbor as thyself."

Here are some important things to consider:

1. If your opinions are important, then so are your neighbors. That doesn't mean we all have to agree. It means we all get to be heard and understood.
2. Listen with your heart as well as your ears.
3. Find the good parts about someone's opinion.
4. Be sincere about trying to understand and learn from a different opinion.

101

So many times when opinions are expressed, we get a hard heart and want *our* opinion to prevail. We need to open up our hearts to have courageous, honest, and thoughtful conversations, instead of discounting each other's opinions.

The Right Message. The Right Person.

Sorting through the mess can also cut down on gossiping, whether that is in the workplace, neighborhoods, families, or with friends. Having the right message with the right person is one way to stop any gossiping conversations.

Often, finding the right message is about having a clear and honest conversation with yourself; first, to determine what and how to say something and with whom. Only then, take the right conversation to the right person.

Example #1 of a Mess: At work, you approach John and ask him why Susan is always late. John doesn't know but assumes she doesn't know how to manage her time. Now, every time she is late, you tell the other coworkers that she doesn't know how to manage her time. That could affect the way they think about her.

Example of Sorting Through the Mess: You approach Susan one day, and being thoughtful about your message, you ask how she is doing. She says fine, but wonders why you are asking. You gently say you notice she is late a lot and wonder if you could help her with anything. She admits to you that she has chronic migraine headaches and that mornings are especially challenging, and she is trying to get to work on time.

Is there a mess here, or just the need for better understanding?

Example #2 of a Mess: You come home from work, and your teenage daughter is grouchy. You ask your spouse what is wrong with her. Your spouse doesn't know but says she must have had a bad day at school. You think she needs to grow up and get over it and not be grouchy. This makes you grouchy and that makes your spouse grouchy and now everyone is in a lousy mood for dinner. See the mess?

Example of Sorting Through the Mess: You come home from work, and your teenage daughter is grouchy. After taking a few minutes to unwind and take care of yourself, you find a moment to talk to your daughter privately. You mention how glad you are to be home from a hard day at work, and you were wondering how her day went. She doesn't feel like talking, but you let her know that you are here for her. You stay in a good mood and are not affected by her bad mood. Later that night, she opens up to you about a problem with her best friend. Did it matter that you had the conversation with the right person?

The mess always comes when we are not talking to the right person about the right thing. In certain core accountability trainings, this is called "Taking it to the source." Other people don't need to be involved when it's the right person having the right conversation with the other right person.

Moving Past Blame and Defending

One time, I was leading a discussion on this concept of "Whose Mess Is It Anyway?" when one lady raised her hand and began to explain her frustrating situation. Every time this lady's mother came over to her house, the mother would get upset because of how messy the house was. This caused Janice to get upset because the mother was upset, and a conversation would ensue, based on both of them being upset.

We probably all know how it went; it was a game of blame and defense. I thanked her for her vulnerability in sharing. (The mother was not present, by the way.) Then, as a group, we worked through this situation with her.

Janice was very much aware that the house was chaotic. She had five daughters, and they were in the thick of very busy schedules. That meant she was a taxi driver, academic and sports supporter, cook, counselor, and chief bottle washer came in last. "I wish it were different," she admitted, "but I'm doing the best I can, and I'm okay with the messy house. However, when my mother comes over, she thinks so differently and wants me to do more to keep the house clean!"

So whose mess is it? (Not the house, the problem.)

We concluded that Janice was in charge of her own mess, as in how she felt about the house. The mother was in charge of *her* mess, as in how she felt about her daughter's house when she came over. They did not need to swap responsibilities; in other words, the daughter did not need to be in charge of how her mother felt, and the mother should not expect her daughter to feel how she felt!

At the end of the day, there were two choices: the blame-game conversation or one of understanding and acceptance.

It does matter! As you get better with yourself and assign healthy accountability, you will get better at sorting through the mess. It takes time, thoughtfulness, and practice . . . and then some.

The Gift in Messes

Messes do not have to be a bad thing. Messes can be opportunities. They can also have pleasant surprises and good outcomes.

Do you want to know the secret to finding them?

It is all in how we sort through them.

- A messy kitchen can produce a beautiful cake.
- A messy bedroom can produce an elated child who has found their shoe.
- A messy office can help to finalize a creative idea.
- A messy parenting problem can bring about a fantastic parenting class.
- Messy finances can bring about creative ideas to solve the fiscal problem.
- A messy relationship can teach you a lot about yourself!

Why Is Sorting Through the Mess Important?

Our conversations need to be rid of distractions and anything else— including judgments—that does not serve us well. We need to stop and focus on the appropriate message with the right person. By doing this, we will have more conversations that are helpful instead of harmful.

Purple CHAT Questions:

1. Do I recognize my own messes?
2. Do I give my messes to someone else?
3. Am I part of the mess or part of the solution?

— 12 —

Building Bridges:
A Better Way for Everybody

*"To effectively communicate, we must realize that we are
all different in the way we perceive the world and use this
understanding as a guide to our communication with others."*
–Tony Robbins

O ur conversations can sometimes go like a dog chasing its tail. How? We go round and round and don't get anywhere until finally we are too tired and give up.

Why do we *chase* conversations? Could it be that we are after one thing and one thing only: our own tails? All we care about is our message and *being right*. Notice, I did not say the "right message." I said, "being right." There is a difference.

We certainly want people to hear and understand our message, but let's face it, so does everyone else. We end up doing what Stephen R. Covey says when he explains, "People don't listen to understand. They listen to reply. The collective monologue is everyone talking and no one listening." See? Round and round, chasing our own tails.

We have all been in conversations where we ended up at the same place that we started. There was a lot of talk, but no clear direction, and both parties were clearly frustrated. Think about it. Did either party stop to ask for any kind of clarification on what was being said? Was either party willing to change their words or their tone? If the answer is no, then "being right" far outweighed wanting to be understood by both parties. Whenever this happens, relationships deteriorate, because "being right" becomes more important than connecting, no matter how good the message was! A message doesn't mean anything if it is not received well. You can shout all you want, but if it falls on deaf ears, nothing is accomplished. A good message is worth putting aside your ego in exchange for understanding and connection. And who knows? You might just change your world.

In today's world, it helps to remember one simple truth: we all want to be understood. It's just human nature. So, a great way to begin a better conversation is to show that you're willing to understand the other person.

When Fear Drives the Conversation

In this contentious world we find ourselves in, our conversations are sometimes driven by fear:

- We fear that we are not being heard.
- We fear that someone else is right and we are wrong.
- We fear that to understand someone means we agree with them.
- We choose fear over understanding.

I like this quote by Marie Curie, a Nobel Prize recipient in 1911. She was a physicist who did pioneering research in radioactivity and more, but what I love about her was that she was very much into discovering things instead of fearing them. She survived World War I and the volatile years following. See if this perspective makes a difference in your conversations:

> "Nothing in life is to be feared,
> It is only to be understood
> Now is the time to understand more,
> So that we may fear less."

These days, everywhere we look, fear shows up more often than understanding. And fear has a way of dividing us. It feels like we're surrounded by rivers of separation—constantly swimming in some form of it.

Here's a case in point: In a more recent period of history in the United States, division was rampant and sides were dramatically drawn with supporters of Biden against Trump. Black Lives Matter against All Lives Matter. Mandatory pandemic masks against no masks. Police force against defund the police, freedom of speech against cancel culture, and LGBTQ against straight, to name a few of the most divisive "sides" from which people felt forced to pick.

Throughout history, movements like the Civil War, women's rights, and the fight against segregation brought powerful change and progress. Yet beneath these efforts, the human need to "be right" has often created an unintended consequence—people standing against people.

Even today, we still face deeply polarizing issues that divide us into sides. And these divisions aren't limited to society at large—they quietly find their way into our personal lives too. Sometimes it becomes *me against my boss, my spouse, my teenager, my neighbor,* or anyone whose view challenges my own.

We all fear, to some degree or another, any one of these sides. Do we know why? Let's slow down and look at it for a moment. Could it be that we don't try to understand the other side? In the heat of a moment or a movement, we forget that people on each side have their own experiences. While they may not be the same as ours, we often talk like we *know* what each other is experiencing.

Building Bridges

A Native American proverb states, "Never judge a man until you've walked a mile in his moccasins." We have probably heard that same thing said one way or another, but that is just it, we may hear it, but do we understand the significance of living this wise counsel? Or the consequences of not living it? The world today is quick to judge without pausing to consider the experiences and challenges that have shaped another person's life.

It's far too easy to offer opinions and act as if we understand another person's story—until we find ourselves on the receiving end of false judgments.

These words from an excerpt of the poem by Mary L. Lathrap help us more fully feel this concept with our hearts and not just run it through our minds:

Judge Softly[3]

"Pray, don't find fault with the man that limps,
Or stumbles along the road.
Unless you have worn the moccasins he wears,
Or stumbled beneath the same load.

There may be tears in his soles that hurt

---

[3] Lathrap, Mary T. The Poems and Written Addresses of Mary T. Lathrap : with a Short Sketch of Her Life. c1895. Retrieved from the Digital Public Library of America, http://catalog.hathitrust.org/Record/002817189. (Accessed September 30, 2025.)

Though hidden away from view.
The burden he bears placed on your back
May cause you to stumble and fall, too.

Don't sneer at the man who is down today
Unless you have felt the same blow
That caused his fall or felt the shame
That only the fallen know.

You may be strong, but still the blows
That were his, unknown to you in the same way,
May cause you to stagger and fall, too.

If we are drowning in rivers of division, we need a pathway. We need bridges of understanding so we don't have to swim in divisiveness. Bridges help us go freely from one side to the other without harming one another. Bridges can be started by one courageous person and built by a unified community. Just one person can start a bridge by being kind, understanding, inclusive, or just willing to listen. When one person takes the first step, it starts a path for others to follow. The question is, will you have the courage to be the one?

Here is a story of one person choosing to build a bridge of understanding. A family in California had some food and other items stolen out of their garage. It happened twice. The mother (Xan), of course, was filled with a lot of anxiety and fear. Before Xan acted on those feelings, she paused and took time to talk with other people about the situation. She received all kinds of different opinions, and because of that, she gained some understanding she didn't have before.

Xan decided to treat the situation with a feeling of charity instead of fear and anger. She thought that if someone needed to steal food out of her garage, there must be people in her neighborhood and the surrounding area who needed food. She started a neighborhood food bin. She put a small bin outside by a tree and filled it full of food. People took food, but interestingly enough, she noticed some people put food in the bin as well. Over time, the little bin needed to be replaced by a bigger container, because more and more people were helping out with supplying food.

This mother took a not-so-good experience and turned it into a meaningful experience of service for her family and their community.

She built a bridge, and then others joined in. She probably didn't have conversations with anybody who took or donated food, but hearts were still connected. People caring for people.[4]

When I think of building bridges, I think of what God has said in the Bible verse, "For God hath not given us the spirit of fear, but of power, and of love and a sound mind," (2 Timothy 1:7).

Nothing in that scripture says we have to give in to the other side, or that we all have to think the same way. It says we are given "a sound mind." That could mean wisdom, discernment, good judgement and perhaps most importantly self-discipline. While I will let you discover what a sound mind means to you, I know this: God gives us the power to choose goodness. He gives us the ability to love both our neighbor and ourselves. And He gives us a mind—not just to think, but to use for good. Perfect skills for building bridges.

Power. We have the power to choose, so let's choose wisely. Choose not to be offended. Choose to learn. Choose to listen. And choose to be responsible for ourselves.

Love. Who doesn't want to be loved? We all do. Start by learning to love yourself and then love others the same way. Love makes the world go round! I know that is cliché, but think about it for a minute. How differently would the world look and operate if we all felt some kind of love? It would be transformational! We all want to be recognized and valued. Love means looking for the good in each other, not what is different or even what unites us, but what is good.

A Sound Mind. Let's use our thinking ability. Although there can be a strong debate on what is right and what is wrong, we all know, deep down inside ourselves, right from wrong. The problem is, we often don't want to go deep inside to figure it out. It's less work to stay shallow and impulsive. Thomas S. Monson, late president of The Church of Jesus Christ of Latter-day Saints, said, "May we ever choose the harder right, instead of the easier wrong." Our hearts will help us if we listen to them.

We can build bridges of understanding in our personal lives and the world around us with these skills. Our relationships are worth the effort. I hear people complaining about the divisiveness all around us, and yet it's the complaining that prevents bridges from being built.

---

[4] https://newsroom.churchofjesuschrist.org/article/how-a-theft-led-one-family-to-create-a-free-food-locker-for-the-hungry)

Complaining does not put us on a good path. When we complain, we are actually putting up walls that block our ability to take action.

In addition, it's vital to recognize the condition of our hearts when we are complaining. Hard hearts make for a hard life. What would happen if we softened and stopped complaining? We might actually see a way to build a bridge from where we are to where we want to be.

Understanding is at the root of finding solutions to difficult conversations. How can we find a solution to something we don't understand? How many times do we go round and round chasing our own tails because we don't understand? It happens all the time. We are not understanding each other, and a lot of the time even ourselves. Understanding means gaining an awareness of the intended meaning or message. Do we go into conversations with *that* goal in mind?

Hardening our hearts and not wanting to understand fuels division in our relationships.We go into a conversation looking to take issue with something and end up ignoring the point of the message. We get uncomfortable when someone else has a different opinion, and so instead of seeking understanding, we sometimes verbally attack them and their beliefs. None of us would ever want this to happen to us, so let's not be doing it to others.

Here is how Gary Chapman, an author and keynote speaker describes this dilemma, "When people respond too quickly, they often respond to the wrong issue. Listening helps us focus on the heart of the conflict. When we listen, understand, and respect each other's ideas, we can then find a solution in which both of us are winners."

Well, there you go. He just built a learning bridge with his words.

Building bridges of understanding happens when we stop looking at people who have different viewpoints from us as being wrong, and start looking for the good parts they have to bring to our relationships, our community, and to society.

We need the perspective of both sides of the conversation:
- Building bridges happens when we can get past being uncomfortable with different messages.
- Building bridges happens when we stop looking for an issue with the message and instead focus on the meaning.
- Building bridges happens when we put ourselves in someone else's shoes.
- Building bridges happens when we recognize that someone else's

insight is just as valuable as ours.

Why Is Choosing to Understand Important to Building Bridges?

Because understanding helps you build bridges where there are none. Build them with caring hearts. Remember, if we want to be understood by others, we need to return the favor and seek to understand them. If you listen with your heart, what will you hear?

Purple CHAT Questions:

1. Who do I need to build a bridge of understanding with?
2. What conversations do I have that would be different with more
3. understanding from me?
4. What do I fear that hinders me from greater understanding?

Part III: BETTER WORDS

Create Your World

"Kind words do not cost much. Yet they accomplish much."
—Blaise Pascal

— 13 —

Are You Truly Breathing?
Getting Unstuck from the Mundane

*"Communication is your ticket to success, if you
pay attention and learn to do it effectively."*
—Theo Gold

" Just breathe!" Has anyone ever said that to you?

You overexerted when exercising. "Just breathe!" You are in a lot of pain. "Just breathe!" You are hysterical over something. "Breathe, sweetheart." Your anger is rising. "Keep breathing."

Why do we say these phrases about breathing when things are not going well? It's funny, but do you ever hear someone say "Breathe" when you feel good or when eating a hamburger? No, because you are in a "controlled state" that is part of your everyday routine. But when things are going wrong, we end up reminding each other just how vital it is to take a breath.

So here's the thing. We don't think of the way we breathe when we are in our mundane routine. It is only when we are on either side of the mundane, either in a crisis or in a state of heightened mindfulness, that we hear "just breathe." If breathing is good for our bodies to get in control, then why not for our conversations? To get control.

Still, the question remains: *are we really breathing?*

Sure, we all do it. The second you left your mother's womb and the umbilical cord was cut, you *had* to breathe on your own or perish. Breathing is the first thing we do coming into this world, and the last thing we stop doing when we leave. It's part of the mortal experience, a natural process of the body and the brain. It's so natural that we don't have to command our body to do it; it just *does it*. We have it on autopilot. Our breathing even adjusts when we are exercising and need to breathe faster, and listens to our command to calm down when it's vital to relax. Breathing is a necessity of life that we rarely have to think about.

Breath Is Life

The funny thing is that if you talk to respiratory therapists, those who specialize in knowing all about breathing, they will tell you that even though breathing is a natural occurrence, there is a right and wrong way to breathe for optimal health. Isn't that fascinating? We don't usually think about that and simply let habit take over.

One summer at a family gathering, I found myself in the kitchen talking to my brother-in-law about life when the topic of breathing came up. As the conversation geek in the family, I was telling him how I have concluded that our conversations are a lot like breathing; simply on autopilot. "We have conversations without putting much thought into them at all," I commented. He nodded.

Rob had recently taken up the sport of road-bike racing. Having switched from riding on the back of a horse for decades to riding on the seat of a bike, he was loving it! Serious about biking, he was excited that he had joined a group that was training for an upcoming road race, but he said he had reached a plateau in his training—basically a ceiling. While he was getting much stronger mentally and physically, he was being limited by his cardio. His breathing just could not keep up with the rest of him. Wanting to overcome his limitation, he went searching for answers. He finally found a useful resource on a YouTube video. From this video, he learned exactly what he needed to do to get the results he wanted.

Here is how Rob described what he learned:

> *"Turns out I was breathing shallow, not using or developing the full capacity of my lungs. The concept made sense, but oh my hell! It was difficult to change or to learn to breathe differently than I'd been doing my whole life. I started to see and experience marked improvements in my stamina and endurance as I practiced breathing fully.*
>
> *It's basically controlling your breath; inhaling and exhaling completely. Inhale: air goes way down deep in your diaphragm—stomach distends. Exhale: air is released completely, causing the stomach to deflate/contract.*
>
> *It was . . . awkward, and I had to really exaggerate the motion until it finally started to become more natural and ultimately almost second nature. I can't tell you how many miles*

and how many hours it has taken. Something I still work on and practice when I am riding."

His results changed remarkably when he came off autopilot and became fully present in the act of breathing.

Breathing Applies in Conversations

Okay, dear reader, here we go. Believe it or not, this directly ties into conversations. Most of our conversations are just like our breathing? On autopilot and underutilized. Don't we just let our learned process take over and not give it much thought? Then we say to ourselves:

"Why are my relationships deteriorating?"

"Why don't I like myself?"

"Why is work not going well?"

"Why have I hit a plateau in my life?"

"What is missing?"

Sure, the natural, not-have-to-think-about-it talking process can work sometimes. But what about the times when we need to do better and *be* better with conversations? The times when we need to have courageous, honest, and thoughtful conversations. As you can see, the whole breathing dilemma mirrors the dilemma we have with conversations—our "natural" and learned behaviors in speaking will not allow us to improve our conversations until we choose to get unstuck.

My brother-in-law not only learned a better way to breathe to help his bike racing, but he also learned a great new life skill that he is applying to many facets of his life. Too good to leave out, he added:

> *"The significance to me personally is the FACT that most, if not all, of what we learn or become good at takes a tremendous, continuous, sustained effort and practice, which includes epic fails. People like to say, 'it's easy for you,' or 'you're naturally thin,' or 'you were just born that way.' It ain't magic and there's nothing easy about it. We become good at something because it's important to us. After all, we work at it . . . We practice."*

This may not be new to you. This life lesson has been said in a million different ways. But we forget and we forget and we forget. We want to change, we want to do better, we want better relationships, we want life to be easier, but we forget. We forget that it takes tremendous, continuous, sustained effort.

As I have talked to people over the years about my passion for better conversations, people will say to me, "Oh, it's so easy for you to have conversations, you are a natural at it," or "You are lucky to have good self-esteem." I want to strongly announce like my brother-in-law, "THERE IS NOTHING EASY ABOUT IT!" I have put in the blood, sweat, and tears, and then more tears. I have done the unpopular things. I have dared to be different, and I have made difficult choices. It has been hard, but it has been important to me. I have chosen to say courageous, honest, and thoughtful words instead of the typical ones.

This includes speaking up when other people just want to avoid the conversation. I have chosen to be uncomfortable in approaching someone to apologize for something I said. I have chosen to look at things from a different perspective and have my words reflect that. I have given up popular things like watching TV, trendy music, and scrolling through social media so I can learn from, listen to, and nurture my relationship with myself, God, and others.

This is not a sacrifice; I gave up certain things for better things. I worked at it and continue to work at it. The beauty is, it gets easier and more enjoyable, and I love it! I love what I am finding off the beaten path of conversations that are on autopilot. Amazement awaits you too!

Now if you're thinking you can't ever have the same response or say the same words, that's not what this is about. Autopilot is talking *without thinking* about what you are saying. It's a habit of not being intentional or talking without heart.

For example, how much intention do you typically have when greeting a colleague at work every day and saying, "Hi, how are you?" This is only a cultural greeting—especially when we don't even wait for the answer, and we are on to the next sentence of our conversation.

While this is often appropriate, if you want to connect hearts and have relationships, your greetings can be more intentional and heartfelt. For example, you could say it at a slower pace and purposefully take a minute to hear the response. We all know the difference in how to say this greeting, so it is meaningful or not. I wonder what the reaction would be if you truly stood still and looked at the other person, waiting for their response. It would be interesting. They might even think that you care.

Here's my invitation: let's take breathing and talking off autopilot!

Let's learn to do both of them better and with more focus and reap the rewards.

Breathing Brings Us to God

The subject of breathing is not just to prove a point in having conversations. It is much deeper than that. Intentional breathing brings us back to God, the one who gave us life's breath.

The Bible has many scriptures discussing this. Here is one of them, "Behold I will cause breath to enter into you and ye shall live,"(Ezekiel 37.5).

Understanding the significance of *breath* draws us back to God each time we inhale the life He has given us. The "breath of life," recognized in many faith traditions, symbolizes a divine spark—a vital force that awakens our spirit and keeps us connected to something greater than ourselves. It invites us into mindful awareness of the miracle of life, and of the many elements lovingly created for our support and well-being.

So how does this sacred breath relate to your new and ongoing Purple CHATs?

Take five minutes—or more—to breathe deeply and slowly, with intention. As you do, gently ask yourself: *Where does my breath come from? What is it inviting me to notice?*

Keep breathing, slow and deep, only concentrating on your breath. You may find that your soul, your higher self, speaks louder than the chatter in your head when you do this. Wisdom will show up. Peace will find a place. And over time, with practice, you will come to know you are not alone.

As we talked about earlier, God is in our journey. God makes our every moment possible because He gives us this gift, the "breath of life." He who gave us life certainly would want to help us *with* life. Thus, breath is vital, not only for getting unstuck in how we communicate, but also in helping us physically reconnect back to God for a more centered, intentional, grateful, and joy-filled life.

Why Is Breathing Better Important?

There are many medical reasons why healthy breathing is vital to our physical, mental, and emotional well-being. But when we bring mindful breathing into our conversations, it becomes even more powerful. It can calm our nerves, sharpen our focus, and create that brief yet powerful pause between react and response—a moment where intention can lead the way instead of defensiveness or impulse. Equally important, mindful breathing gives us the gift of space—space to listen, to understand, and to respond. Each deep, intentional breath nourishes the body, energizing the heart and brain alike giving us the best chance at having heartfelt connections.

Purple CHAT Questions:

1. What aspects of my life are on autopilot?
2. How would breathing change my conversations?
3. How would my relationships be different if I was fully present?

14

The Art of Communicating: Creating with Words

*"The difference between the right word and
the almost right word is the difference
between lightning and a lightning bug."*
—Mark Twain

I was at lunch one afternoon with several friends. It was someone's birthday, and we tried to put aside our hectic lives with children and running a household to celebrate. It was just a couple of hours sitting in a restaurant renewing friendships. One or more of us even had a new baby to bring along. We were involved in our life discussions when one of them shared that she had been having chronic headaches, but when she'd changed one of her medications, the headaches stopped.

Well, there could have been a blaring light in front of me, and it wouldn't have been as dramatic as the light that just went off in my head! Without moving or saying a thing, I was deeply involved in my thought that maybe the medication I was taking was contributing to my depression at the time. Wow, what a thought! I couldn't wait to get home. I called my doctor, got the medication changed, and it made a tremendous difference in my life. I don't think my friend has any idea that what she said was life-changing for me. That was a big wake-up call to me about two things. We need interaction with each other . . . and words matter.

Another conversation with a family member went differently. In talking about a certain topic, she disbelievingly could not understand how I could be "so naive." I know she wasn't trying to be mean, but I remembered that word "naive," and it caused me to often ask myself if I truly knew anything about the world.

Have you ever had a conversation where someone said something that lit up your mind—a lightbulb moment you'll never forget? Or maybe someone said something that was deeply hurtful and that stuck with you just as much. I have had plenty of them, as I know you have. Some of them end up in laughter, and some end up in tears or even fear.

We all know the saying: *"Sticks and stones may break my bones, but words can never hurt me."* But the truth is, words *do* stick. Sometimes for a lifetime.

Words matter. They shape the way we see ourselves, the way we relate to others, and the way we experience the world. They build us and others up—or tear us down. They echo long after they're spoken.

Just like an artist practices their craft to create beauty that others can see and feel, we too are artists through our conversations. Every word has the power to connect, heal, inspire, and even transform someone's world.

Since none of us is perfect, this is not about having the perfect thing to say; it's about the intentions behind the words. With thought and practice, we can all learn to speak in ways that build deeper, more meaningful connections from the heart.

My passion for writing this book started when I discovered I could be creative with words. I learned, firsthand, that there is an *art* to communicating. But just like painting, sculpting, music, and dance, you have to immerse yourself in it to see and understand the artistry that exists and what is possible for you, in your own, unique expression.

As I mentioned earlier in the book, there was a time in my communication when I had reached an all-time low with my daughter. Surprisingly enough, when she spoke the words "shut up" to me, that all-time low turned into my all-time high because I was about to learn the art of communicating.

As it turns out, there was a lot more to the story. Unbeknownst to me, my daughter was equally as upset as I was, and by the time she arrived at school, she went to her school counselor and spilled the beans about what had happened at home. Sometime during that day, the school counselor called me. She shared that my daughter had been in to talk to her, extremely upset and feeling bad. The counselor and I talked for a while, and then she kindly invited me to a parenting class called "Parenting with Love and Logic." I was all in.

Blessed be the day that school counselor called me, because as you know, attending that parenting class was life-changing for me! I will forever be thankful to her for the way she showed up to that conversation and graciously, kindly helped a wounded mother find her way to a better relationship with her daughter, and ultimately with herself and others.

The parenting class was a six-week course. I loved every minute of it so much that I took the course a second time, dragging some friends along with me. It taught me that words do matter: Pick lousy words–send a lousy message. Pick confrontational words–you'll get a confrontation. Pick positive words– you just might have everyone working together!

We can choose better words. Like an artist, carefully select a color palette and begin with an outline and intention. When we choose better words, we send a more beautiful message, often with a better outcome.

In the beginning, I had to ask the hard questions, like:

"Are my words helping or hurting?"

"Am I conveying the message that is in my heart with my words?"

"Are my relationships getting better because of my words?"

Well, my answers were not what I wanted them to be. I discovered I didn't like the way I was doing things. I certainly didn't like how heavy parenting felt and the conversations I was having. I knew I was going in the wrong direction.

What opened up my world was learning that I could pick the right words, in the right order, to create the right message. There truly was an art to communicating! It wasn't just a bunch of words with punctuation at the end. *Words can create! And,* I thought, *maybe they can create a beautiful message, a vision, an emotion, and priceless relationship*s.

This idea felt unfamiliar to me. I had always thought of creating with colors, fabric, canvas, paint, wood, clay, or glass—but not with words. I wasn't completely sure what it meant, but I was sure of one thing: I didn't want to keep living my life the same way, repeating the same patterns over and over.

Life had begun to feel heavy—like I was stuck in trenches that I had dug myself through my mindset, my actions, and yes, my words. I knew I was reacting on autopilot: when the kids didn't do what I thought they should, when finances were tight and the bills needed to be paid, or when something unexpected and unwanted showed up in my day.

My solution was always the same: try harder to control it. I relied on logic, rules, and a sense of power I thought I had—believing that if I could control people and situations, then I could control my life. But it obviously wasn't working. Because the more I tried to control, the more miserable I became.

That's when I decided to give it a shot. I would experiment with better words.

I started putting into practice all the skills I'd learned in class, and immediately, I felt lighter! No longer was parenting heavy; it was enjoyable! I was becoming better at communicating. I was being lifted out of the trenches.

Words are actually changing my world, I marveled one day. The knowledge I gained helped me notice everything around me in a more meaningful way. I was better-equipped to create more meaningful relationships in my life.

Years after the parenting class, I was still fascinated with the artistry of words—so much so that when I went back to school to finish my degree I changed my major from accounting to communication.

One of my first eye-opening experiences with words happened at work. The office ordered lunch one day for everybody, and somehow I got skipped. When the food came, there was nothing for me. My boss felt bad. I didn't because I had control of my happiness. That day, I happened to have brought lunch! I was fine with eating my food.

In his attempt to make things better, however, my boss offered me the money that he would have spent on my lunch. "Please take the money," he said.

I declined the money because I didn't need it to make me feel better. "No, thank you."

"Please take the money, Dezlee."

"No, thank you," I declined again. "I promise you, I don't need it."

But oh boy, it was getting a little tense in the office. Once more he tried, but this time he added two words:

"Please take the money *for me.*"

All of a sudden, the whole meaning of the conversation changed. Immediately, I said, "Sure, I can do that for you."

See, I could take the money to help him feel better; I simply hadn't needed to do it for myself. Those two words made a big difference in the message. The whole situation—and the words—were truly a game changer for me. I thought, *how interesting the impact that two words could have on a sentence, in a conversation, and ultimately on an outcome.* I suddenly became even more fascinated by words.

I took that experience and applied it to other conversations. In parenting, I changed the picture from, "Hey, I am in charge" to "Hey, I care about you and want to help you succeed." I went from saying, "That makes me mad" or "Why didn't you do what I said?" to "I'm sorry, how do you feel about that?" or "What can I do to help you?"

At work, I went from joining in the bad conversations to creating good ones. Instead of talking *about* people, I decided to talk *to* people and resolve uncomfortable situations. A step at a time, I became more creative and more intentional. Just like words changed the atmosphere in my home and even between my husband and me, it was changing the bigger world wherever I went, in small and big ways.

How Can I Make Your Day Better?

Creating with words does not have to be a big production. In fact, it only takes a word or two to completely change things around. One of my favorite stories about using the right words to change hearts was written by NYT best-selling author Richard Paul Evans. He put a story on his blog and encouraged everyone to share it.

Richard told the story of how he and his wife, Kerri, always struggled in their marriage. Over time, it had become unbearable, and they were going to get divorced. He came home from a book tour, and that night, he had an impression of what he needed to do. The next morning, he said to his wife, "How can I make your day better?"

She didn't want to answer, but he insisted, so she said, "Well then, go clean the kitchen." He did!

The next morning, he used the same words, asking, "How can I make your day better?" Again, she didn't want to answer but she did, thinking that he wouldn't do it. She told him to go clean the garage. He did!

After weeks of doing this every day, not only was Richard's heart softened, but hers was too. They started working things out and are still married! It all started because one person was willing to change the conversation to paint a different picture. It went from a picture of "we can't work together" to "let's work together." The words he chose (and his actions to back them), changed their world.

After reading this story, I decided to try using these words myself to see what would happen. No one knew what I had read or what I was doing; I simply started using the words in my conversations. I changed the words slightly to make it more me. I began saying, "What can I do to help you today?"

I made it a point to say it every morning to my husband, Clark. I would say it to friends and coworkers when the occasion arose. An interesting thing happened: I found my heart being softened at times when *I* wanted to be resentful or upset! I felt other people's hearts changing when I spoke those simple words. I saw their expressions, and a different picture was being painted. I was a bit shocked when, after a while, Clark started saying the same words to me. Together, we began to paint a different picture of our relationship. Hearts were softer, words were kinder, and caring was more abundant. Our marriage relationship became less forceful and more authentic. And, I'm happy to report, we are still together.

What kind of artwork do you see on your canvas when you hear these words?

"I need you."
"Hey, why don't you come join us?"
"Help me to understand better."
"What can I help you with?"
"You can do it!"
"You did a great job!"
"I really care about you."
"I'm sorry."

Body Language Matters Too

When we want to create a certain picture with words, we must remember that it's not just the words that matter. Our body language and tone also "color" that picture in powerful ways. In fact, studies show that they often speak louder than our actual words. That's why it's important to make sure our words, tone, and body language are all having the same conversation, because if not, something is going to ruin the picture we thought we were painting.

I am sure we have all been in conversations where the messages were louder and clearer from the body language and tone they used than from their words. You heard one thing but saw another message.

Here is a common conversation that often gets mixed up. The one about being sorry. Somebody catches a mistake we've made at work. We want to say sorry but not really. We say it just so the other person can hear it, and we can be done with the whole situation. Meanwhile, our body is tense, our facial expression is not even close to being sorry, and we walk away abruptly. What did we just communicate?

Here's another example that taught me a lot. When Clark and I would go out to eat, we'd sit in the car, still in the driveway, stuck in this little loop: "You pick." "No, you pick." Finally, Clark would say, "I don't care—wherever you want to go." So I'd choose a place. But then his body language would quietly disagree—his face would get stern, a sigh, or total silence. His words said one thing, but everything else said something completely different.

It wasn't really about where we were going to eat. It was about clarity, honesty, and emotional alignment. Words without matching tone or body language can create confusion, even when we're not trying to be confusing. That's when Purple CHATs came to the rescue. I finally had the courage to bring it up—not to blame, but to understand and to be understood. I gently told him that if he said he didn't care, he needed to show he was okay with my decision. I chose my words thoughtfully, and I approached the conversation with care rather than frustration.

He got it. We both realized that communication isn't just about speaking—it's about matching the message we say with the message we show. And now, when he says he doesn't care, he really means it.

I began to have so much fun with my newfound mindset about creating with words. I learned skills and even subtle techniques like artists do when taking classes. These include listening better, choosing better words, putting words together better, delivering a clearer message, and having more heart in my words. I have experimented, failed, tried again, seen success, and created precious relationships and friendships. Most of all, it has helped me to be the kind of person I want to be, not just wishing I would be! My life is richer and more meaningful as I create with honesty, compassion, understanding, love, thoughtfulness, and courage.

It has taken time. I have learned to encourage more and lecture less. Accept instead of control. Understand instead of needing to be right. Love instead of resentment. Listen more and react less. And have more conversations that matter.

Life doesn't seem so routine anymore. I have come a long way, and look forward to going even further as I engage in heartfelt conversations.

As most artists will tell you, it *does* matter what details you choose when creating a work of art. The color, fabric, metal, paint, design, and tools you choose make a huge difference. So it is in conversations. The words you choose matter. The way you put words together matters. The tone, speed, and body language matter. It *all* matters when you want to create a spectacular work of art or a meaningful conversation.

Tangible Tools for Painting Words

Choose words that help solve problems instead of creating them. Phrases like:

"I know we can figure this out," instead of "You are the one who caused this problem."

How about offering suggestions instead of being right. Try saying: "Here is an idea that might work," instead of "I think you should do it this way."

And my favorite:

"Hey, I don't think I communicated that very well; let me try again."

A lot of practice—that's what it took to change my conversations. It didn't happen automatically. I even used scripts from a parenting class to get started. It reminded me that change begins with our mindset: when we learn to think before we speak, we change what we create with our words.

I started practicing conversations with my kids. At the time, I had four kids, between six and sixteen years old. Boy, did I have a lot of conversations to practice on! Now, don't get me wrong, our conversations were typical, but that's just it; I wanted better ones. When my kids complained about what went wrong at school and all kinds of other difficult stuff, I took a deep breath and said to myself, "Choose different words." Instead of saying things like, "Why did you do that?' and "You should do this" or "Listen to me next time I tell you something," I intentionally chose words like, "How can I help you?" "How did that experience make you feel?' and "I know you will figure it out." I got better as I practiced, and over time, I ended up with better relationships. Life just felt more joyful and invigorating.

I found I loved the creation process. It seemed like a whole new world opened up for me. I became more aware of people, feelings, thoughts, situations, and outcomes.

Why Is Learning the Art of Communicating Important?

If your goal in conversation is to build the kind of relationships you truly want, then communication becomes an art worth practicing. Don't leave your words—or their impact—to chance. Be intentional about what you want to create.

Have you ever been around someone who leaves you feeling uplifted, positive, and motivated after a conversation? Now, contrast that with the person who consistently leaves you feeling frustrated, angry, or down. Which person do you want to be, and what kind of impact do you want to create?

A teacher who taught other teachers often guided his students to become the people they aspired to be. He asked them to draw two circles. In the first, he told them to write the names of people who have hurt, hindered, discouraged, or held them back. In the second, he asked them to write the names of those who have helped, encouraged, inspired, and made a difference in their lives. Then he asked the thought-provoking question, "Which circle do you want your name to appear in to others?"

Purple CHAT Questions:

1. What do I create with my words?
2. Do I like the outcome of my creations in my world and relationships??
3. What kind of person do I want to be, and how can selecting my words more artistically help?

15

Texting Madness:
Check Before You Text

"Of all the life skills available to us, communication
is perhaps the most empowering."
—Bret Morrison

I have to admit, I have had a hard time embracing technology. While I am doing better, it continues to be a battle. Sure, I have heard all the arguments on how great technology is, how it is advancing everything we do, giving us more knowledge and choices. While this is true, I've come to discover that technology has both a good and a bad side to it. I didn't think it was too earth-shattering until cell phones made their debut.

My husband, Clark, and I were right in the middle of raising our kids, when the cell phone craze hit, followed immediately by social media. I had no reason to embrace this new tech. Cell phones were expensive, different, and all I could see was the harm they would do to kids being on phones instead of in front of people. I resisted, big time!

And then one day, Clark bought me a phone, put it in my hand, and simply said, "It's time." I started using it—but not without a fair amount of kicking and screaming. Yes, my choice to delay put me behind in many ways. Some would say I missed out. That's one way to look at it. But as time has passed, I've realized how grateful I am that I didn't let technology consume my life. I look around now and see that for many people, it's a constant balancing act—using technology while still trying to stay connected to who they really are.

Of course, as predicted, the convenience of using a cell phone for calling was wonderful. I caught on to that one pretty fast. When it came to texting, well, *that* was a different story. I felt the need to put my foot down and stick with familiar methods of communicating, such as a phone call or talking face-to-face. It was all changing too fast for me. And I continued to see the consequences of miscommunication.

Texting is the new shorthand method for having conversations, so it's important we talk about it. Texting has its own language and moods and can be so awesome and at the same time so devastating. All I could see, or was willing to see, were the not-so-good parts of texting as it pertained to having a conversation with someone.

For a long time, I felt like we were going backwards in our conversations. People were saying *anything* and assuming *everything* as the conversations went back and forth through texting, much less "auto-correct" text and voice text errors! Texting left out so much of what effective communication needs, which is tone and nonverbal body language. It also put us in a position of being able to hide behind the cell phone screen instead of standing in front of someone to be accountable for what was said.

Texting also gave us more leeway in leaving a conversation; we just didn't have to respond. I, in my attempt to not engage in this type of communicating, or should I say miscommunication, would often push the call button, rather than continue with texting. I thought to myself, *I used to verbally talk to people all the time, and now all we do is text.*

People often say that texting is convenient—and it is. Convenience is quick, easy, and offers many benefits. But sometimes convenience makes it just as easy to give up things that are also good—like putting in effort, being intentional, slowing down, and creating meaningful, healing connections. **Convenience should have a place at the table, but it shouldn't take the place of doing things that matter.**

Our conversations should matter. They help us improve ourselves, strengthen our relationships, and deepen our understanding of each other. But texting can sometimes be too quick and too easy for the kind of conversations that require more heart, more effort, and more presence.

From Texting Madness to Texting Gladness

After years of frustration, I changed my tactics. I have embraced the madness of texting with *gladness*. I decided instead of being annoyed, I would influence the madness by the way I used texting.

I started to experiment. If I was going to have conversations through texting, then my goal was to make them as good as possible. Even great!

Being aware of our texting mannerisms is the first thing we need to do if we want to do better with our texting conversations. Texting has no voice tone. We need to make sure the words we choose give the tone we want to send.

We have all heard the saying, "Think before you speak." Now we should be saying, "Check before you text."

When we slow down just enough to read what we have texted, then we can discover the tone that is in the text. By doing this, we can ask ourselves if changing a few words would change the tone of the message so it's better understood. Remember when we send those texts, there is a lot of assuming that happens because there is no tone or body language. It's crucial to do all we can so the other person receives the right message. Choosing good words in the right order can make the difference in how the message is received. I know that emojis can be used to express body language through texting, and sometimes very effectively! However, be aware that emojis are not appropriate in all conversations, so be wise when you use them.

Here are some examples of words and tones.

Sure. Or,

Sure!

Can you feel the difference in tone? How about with a few extra words:

Sure! I would love to. Or *Sure! I got it!*

None of these are right or wrong; it is about the tone you want to send. Here is another word:

Okay. Or,

Okay! Or,

Okay, I will see you then!

Hopefully, you can see, they each have distinctive or different tones. One more:

No problem. Or,

No problem! Or,

No problem, I can do that!

A little more effort in your text may mean a whole lot more understanding. If things are going badly in your texting conversations, check your tone.

And talking about tone, let's address texting with all caps. In texting language, it conveys strong emotions like shouting or anger. It can also mean urgency or emphasizing a certain emotion. In other words, it can mean different things to different people. Don't assume that the receiver is understanding the message with the same meaning as you sent it. All caps tend to be a rude and offensive way of texting. A wonderful relationship is not worth the misunderstanding of all caps.

Give Yourself Permission to Get Creative

It took me a while, but I finally learned how to communicate a message with something other than texting words. What a whole new world this was! Sometimes the right conversation can happen when sending a song, poem, video, article, or meme through texting. By using these different ways of communicating, the message can be clearer than trying to find words that you sometimes can't find.

For example, a friend told me that her granddaughter sent her a song through text to describe how she was feeling. She suddenly understood clearly what her granddaughter was trying to communicate! It made all the difference in the world.

At Christmas time during the 2020 pandemic, when we were not gathering, I sent a Christmas concert of songs to my siblings as a way of saying, "Merry Christmas, I love you." This became a lifesaver for some of us who were struggling at the time with the whole pandemic situation. Sharing songs, articles, videos, or memes is another way to communicate that you care when words can be hard to feel or dismissed easily.

Voice-Recorded Texts

There is still another great way to communicate with all this technology. Yes, there's more! It's audio text messaging, and it's excellent for conveying a clearer message. To my surprise, I see it as being underutilized. This method is still a text, but you are sending your actual voice that the receiver can hear. This allows you to send a message with your tone and inflection so they can better understand the intended message. Why do I love this? You can be funny, serious, happy, or upset, and they will hear that and not have to assume the mood of your text. For those of us who love to talk and be heard, this is a dream come true! Haha!

But in all seriousness, this is a great way to end those text messages that are sensitive and are not going the right way. Instead, send your voice! And be courageous, honest, and thoughtful when doing it.

Embracing texting and voice texting for the good that they offer has added another dimension to my conversations. This discovery came as I slowed down, became aware of my tone, and intentionally chose certain words. I have turned texting madness into texting gladness. It takes thought and personal responsibility for what you put out there.

Don't let bad texting be part of who you are. Feel good about what you are texting. Or, choose not to do it at times. Just because you can text doesn't mean you have to.

Why Is Texting Important to Communication?

Texting is shaping us and our conversations, so let's use it for good. Sometimes, when a cell phone is between us and the other person, it's easy to turn our hearts off and let our fingers do the talking.

Don't use texting as a weapon of revenge or hurtfulness.

Don't hide behind texting.

Instead, further your conversations because of texting. Let's make sure texting is bringing gladness to our relationships and not madness. Use it wisely and not regretfully. Make your world a better place by having courageous, honest, thoughtful, and creative conversations through texting.

Purple CHAT Questions:

1. Am I aware of the tone in my text conversations?
2. How can I personally and professionally improve my text messages?
3. Does texting bring gladness to me and the other person?

Part IV: SHOWING UP BETTER

Share Your Heart

"It is your heart and your presence that will
make a difference in your conversations."
—Dezlee Hancock

16

Show Up!
Because It Matters!

"To the world you may just be one person.
But to one person you may just be the world."
—Dr. Seuss

Jorge couldn't believe he was sitting across the table from his dad at Sushi Monster, hearing these words. It was only five days before marrying the love of his life, and the person who should have been there like a rock for him was not. Instead, his father was telling him, in no uncertain terms, in front of his soon-to-be wife, how getting married to this girl was wrong and he should call it off. Jorge hadn't been very close with his dad since his parents divorced, and he needed a loving, supportive dad right now. Getting married was exciting and scary at the same time, and he needed someone to be on his team and stand by his side. Unfortunately, his dad just couldn't do it—not monetarily, not emotionally, nor physically. Before he left, his father handed Jorge a one-hundred-dollar bill to help with his tux, but that was all the support that came.

There was a couple who did show up for Jorge, in a big way, with a big heart. Two friends from their church who cared deeply offered Jorge and his new wife a package deal for their honeymoon. On the fly, they gladly shared free sky miles and a timeshare they had in Hawaii. The newly married couple couldn't believe it! For someone to give so generously with such love was overwhelming. They didn't know what to do except graciously accept the gift and vow to be someone who would show up for others when it mattered.

Showing up: does it really matter?

Maybe the better question is: *Does it matter when we don't show up?* And before we answer that, we need to ask—*what does "showing up" actually mean?*

To show up means more than simply being physically present. It means bringing our attention, our presence, and our caring to someone or something. Purple CHATs takes this concept even further—it invites us to show up not just with our bodies, but also with our words and our hearts.

The challenge we face in today's world is that we are pulled in so many directions. We have endless activities to go to, commitments to tend to , roles to fulfill, and don't forget responsibilities. We get so busy moving from one thing to the next that we often "show up" or fail to show up—without even realizing the impact of that choice.

- Maybe we show up at family gatherings.
- Maybe we show up at work.
- Maybe we show up at the dinner table.
- Maybe we show up at a party.
- Maybe we show up at a friend's house.
- Maybe we show up at a funeral.
- Maybe we show up at church.
- Maybe we show up at school.
- Maybe we show up at a sporting event.
- Maybe we show up for someone in need.

Showing up isn't just about filling a seat or standing in a room. When we leave our hearts at home, we're only offering half of what really matters. So when we show up—for an event, for a conversation, or for someone—we need to bring more than just our bodies. We need to bring our hearts too.

Let's be honest. A lot of times we show up just because we feel we have to, out of obligation, duty, or even guilt. And when that's the reason, think about what we carry in our hearts. We might feel annoyed, resentful, inconvenienced, or even defensive.

But when we choose to show up because it matters—because it's meaningful, fun, or helpful—we come with a different kind of heart, don't we? We're more open, more willing, and more present. We're there for others as well as for ourselves. That's when the good stuff happens. When we show up with full, open hearts, we connect. Our presence blends our hearts with others, and that benefits everyone.

Finding Balance in "Showing Up"

Life has a whole list of things to "show up" to. It is unrealistic to think we can show up to everything, every time, because we simply can't. But when we do choose to be present, the more important question becomes: *how* are we showing up?

We can't always show up in person, and that's okay. We can still connect through a call, a text, a Zoom chat, or even a handwritten note. In those moments, engaging our hearts matters most—because heartfelt words can make a real difference, even from a distance.

Life gives us endless opportunities to "show up," but we all know we can't be everywhere all the time. So the real question isn't *can* we show up—but *how* we show up when we do.

- Do you ever show up to an event and immediately start judging how others have shown up? "Wow, she's grouchy today." "He's so full of himself. "She's always late."
  "They never talk to anyone." Have you ever thought about what people might say about how *you* show up? A little grace goes a long way—you may find you need some too.
- Do we pay attention to how we are showing up? Did we arrive on time? Did we check our own emotions and ego at the door? Are we contributing or draining the energy in the room? Did we choose to engage in conversation and help someone else who is feeling shy or awkward?
- Do our cell phone habits keep us from showing up fully? It's easy to think of our phones as an extension of ourselves because they are always with us, but remember: they don't have a heart. And when our attention is constantly divided between the screen and the person in front of us, real conversations simply can't happen. So ask yourself: how would you feel if someone treated you the same way—choosing their phone over your presence? Try less phone focus and more people curious.

If the way other people show up affects you, then remember how you show up can affect other people too.

I'm not suggesting we have to be perfect—because we don't. Perfection isn't possible. But what *is* possible, and deeply important, is being mindful of how we show up in the world and recognizing the impact that has on others and on ourselves.

Sometimes we avoid showing up because of people. Someone might skip a funeral or a wedding just to avoid a certain family member. Another person might stop going to church because of how someone there treats them. And some people even start showing up late to work meetings because they feel dismissed or disrespected by their boss.

The truth is, relationships are messy. Human connection can be uncomfortable, unpredictable, and sometimes painful. But it's also essential for a meaningful and beautiful life.

Mother Teresa of Calcutta captured this truth in a poem (originally written by Kent Keith) that hung on the wall where she carried out her life's work. It expresses this idea perfectly.

Do It Anyway[5]

People are illogical, unreasonable, and self-centered;
love them anyway.
If you do good, people may accuse you
of selfish, ulterior motives;
do good anyway.
If you are successful, you will win
false friends, true enemies;
succeed anyway.
The good you do today will be forgotten tomorrow;
do good anyway.
Honesty and frankness make you vulnerable;
be honest and frank anyway.
The biggest men and women with the biggest
ideas can be shot down by the smallest men
and women with the smallest minds;
think big anyway
People favor underdogs but follow only top dogs;
fight for a few underdogs anyway
What you spend years building, may
be destroyed overnight;
build anyway.

---

[5] Commandments by Kent M. Keith.

**People really need help but may attack
you if you do help them;**
help people anyway
**Give the world the best you have, and
you'll get kicked in the teeth;**
give the world the best you've got anyway.

Oh, that takes a moment to think about! There is a lot of self-reflection in those words. Maybe there is something there that will inspire you.

Here's the crucial part: we must decide not to let others determine how we show up or whether we show up at all. When we do, we hand over our power. That not only drains our passion, but it can also dull our sense of purpose. Allowing someone else to have that much influence weakens our sense of self. **Show up because *you* choose to— because that's who you are.**

In going back to our previous examples, maybe you might think about them a little differently:

1. If you've been skipping family weddings, reunions, funerals, or good old holiday parties because certain people rub you the wrong way, remember, don't become that person yourself. And don't let their behavior keep you from showing up for the loved ones who truly matter to you. Go, be present, and choose to have a great time.

2. When others dominate conversations and only talk about themselves, you can still show up with curiosity and kindness. Ask others how *they* are doing. As Dale Carnegie observed, one of the deepest human desires is to feel significant and valued. By helping others feel seen and appreciated, you strengthen your relationships. And if it takes a little (or a lot) of tolerance, that's okay—you can do that when you've taken care of your inner struggles.

3. If you've stopped going to church because of how others behave or judge, don't let that keep you away. If church is important to you, show up, and show others, by example, what it means to worship with grace and love. When others bring judgment, you can bring compassion.

4. And if you dread work meetings because of a negative boss or other's bad attitudes, don't let that energy define you. Choose to

be different. Show up for your coworkers with a positive attitude and an open mind. You might be surprised how your intentional presence can shift the tone for everybody.

When you make the decision to "show up" fully—no matter what others do—you reclaim your power and create space for connection, purpose, and growth.

What Are You Bringing to the Table?

Here's the thing to remember: everyone has a mix of strengths and weaknesses. We all carry our own flaws and abilities, our failures and achievements, regardless of where we are in life. And so, when we show up, so do these aspects of ourselves. For instance, a weakness might appear as arrogance, where we feel the need to assert that we're better than others, or it might show up in taking offense too easily. Weaknesses can also manifest as poor listening, being unwilling to learn, being insensitive, or lacking patience. Narcissists often highlight the weaknesses of others while ignoring their own. Trust me, that's not the approach you want to adopt; it's ultimately harmful.

The great news is that while we all have weaknesses, we also bring strengths to the table. Maybe we're knowledgeable, patient, kind, a good listener, or willing to serve. Whatever it is, we need to bring those strengths with us.! How we show up matters. And if we want others to accept our weaknesses and recognize our strengths, we need to offer the same acceptance and recognition to them. We need to reach out with hearts that help rather than hurt.

A great way to do this is by choosing collaboration over competition. Cheering each other on and staying positive is far more rewarding than being negative. Give it a try; you might just enjoy it!

My husband, Clark, worked in the tennis world, doing everything from teaching and coaching to stringing rackets and running tournaments. It was truly a family affair, as all of our kids were involved as well. Between Clark organizing tournaments and the kids playing, we saw a lot of action. He often said things ran more smoothly when parents weren't around because, more often than not, their presence brought tension and pressure that everyone could sense. He dealt with more poor sportsmanship from parents than from the kids. When parents weren't involved, however, the kids were able to navigate the game on their own and learned how to handle the challenges. It was clear that how parents "showed up" had a direct impact on their kids and the overall atmosphere. That said, other parents encouraged their kids to support and cheer for all the players and to hang out together afterward. Sporting events test our ability to show up.

The "Why Do I" Question

As we grow older, we often lose that innocent sense of curiosity—the instinct to ask "why?" Instead of exploring, we begin to seek control over situations, outcomes, and even over other people. We become more focused on managing life then understanding it. But one of the most powerful ways to show up better—for yourself and for others—is to reclaim that childlike curiosity. And sometimes it starts with being curious about yourself.

Why do I behave this way?
Why do I say those things?
Why do I feel this way?

This isn't about judgment. It's not an interrogation. It's an honest conversation between your mind, your heart, and your soul—a conversation you may have been avoiding for far too long.

Let's bring back a lesson we all learned as kids, one that was meant to keep us safe:

Stop. Look. Listen.

Remember that childhood lesson about safely crossing the street or train tracks? You were told to stop, look, and listen to avoid danger. That same advice applies now, not just to protect yourself, but to avoid hurting others along the way.

If you find yourself in a tough conversation or a moment of tension, **stop.** Take a breath. Pause. There is power in a pause.

Then, **look.** Become aware. What's happening around you? Who's present? What dynamics are in play?

Finally, **listen.** Not just to others but to your inner voice. Your conscience. Your truth. And then ask:

Why do I come home from work already on edge?
Why do I speak so harshly to myself?
Why do I feel distant or resentful to others?
Why do I lose my patience so quickly?

These are not easy questions. But the answers might lead you to a safer, healthier place, mentally and emotionally.

And don't stop there. We must also ask "why" in moments of good times, not just in struggle.

Why do I love my spouse, partner, or friends?
Why do I care about the energy I bring to work?
Why do I offer to help my neighbor?
Why do I find time for myself?

These questions remind us of what matters. They help us stay aligned with our values, our purpose, and our joy. The answers remind us of who we are and who we're becoming.

Take the time to ask. Take the time to listen. Your curiosity could be the very thing that changes everything for you and for those you love.

Power of Presence

If you haven't noticed, our world desperately needs people like you to show up and engage in conversations that truly matter. Ones with the right message, to the right people that build bridges of understanding and solutions.

Through studying people and the art of conversation, I've come to realize that one of the ways we've lost our way is in how we view our "freedom of speech." Yes, it is a right, but even more profoundly, it's a *privilege*.

Let's reframe it this way: it's a privilege to have the right to speak freely.

Unfortunately, many in our society have swapped "privilege" with "entitlement." And when we adopt an entitlement mindset, the way we show up changes completely because the attitude of entitlement is disrespectful, self-indulging, and uncaring.

We need leaders in homes, schools, communities, and countries who know how to truly "show up." Leaders who know that the right to free speech carries with it a responsibility to use it for the betterment of society, and for our own well-being.

Here is a challenge for all of us: to take to heart the profound statement James Madison made as one of the founding fathers of America. "To suppose that any form of government will secure liberty or happiness without any virtue in the people, is a chimerical idea." This should inspire us, not only for our time but for our future generations to promote the quality of virtue.

Why Is Showing Up Important?

If you're ever uncertain about the impact of showing up, think back to a time when someone entered your life—perhaps like Jorge's friends for his wedding—with both their heart *and* presence. Remember how those people profoundly affected you. Some of those people may not even know what they did for you. I have an entire list of people, from a high school counselor to a cherished aunt to a next-door neighbor. Their presence shaped me, and I am passing it on. Showing up truly creates a ripple effect that can change lives for generations to come. Watch what happens!

Purple CHAT Questions:

1. Am I showing up wherever I go, with my heart?
2. How can I affect others more positively by the way I choose to show up?
3. What is a powerful way I can show up in the lives of those I love today?

17

I'm Back!
Being Resilient in Conversations

"The single most important thing [you can do] is to shift [your] internal stance from 'I understand' to 'Help me understand.' Everything else follows from that . . ."
—Douglas Stone

Even though we have talked about a lot of things to make our conversations better, the fact is we can't control it all. There will be difficult conversations no matter what we do, even if we do all the right things. We can be well prepared, and they still will not go as planned. What do we do then? Do we stay or go?

There are people in our lives who need us to be there for them, no matter what. We need to learn to be resilient in having difficult conversations. It is about how to successfully deal with unsuccessful conversations. It can be done.

Meaningful conversations are what moves life along. They help us grow, solve problems, build relationships, and make the world around us better. Everything begins with a conversation—whether it's setting a goal, learning something new, or raising children to be ready for the world.

If we compromise our conversations for any number of reasons, we jeopardize our own progress, as well as society's. Today, we see this happening everywhere: in politics, families, religion, communities, and even within ourselves. We've weakened our conversations not only by the words we choose, but sometimes by avoiding them altogether.

Resilience: Staying in the Game

When I started my personal quest for better conversations, I was intrigued by the challenge of how to *stay* with a really difficult conversation. It was hard! And I failed—a lot. I also learned a lot. What I learned was that being resilient was the key. To build resilience, I would ask myself the following questions: How well did I recover from challenging conversations so that I could get back in the game and make a difference? And if I got back in the game, was I coming back as a *better* player, or was I going to get thrown out again?

Resilience is a crucial life skill. It's the ability to face challenges, grow through them, and keep moving forward. Many conversations, especially those that matter most to our relationships, can be challenging. It's essential to develop resilience in these moments, empowering us to be present and engage thoughtfully, even when the discussion is tough.

We have all encountered conversations that have left us feeling exhausted, frustrated, angry, or any number of other emotions. They happen at work with people who are always negative, or with our teenager who just doesn't seem to "get it." They happen on the phone with someone from customer service who is not giving any kind of customer service. These kinds of conversations often make us not want to engage in any further conversations, even the good ones!

When I am speaking with groups, people so often share that they hate talking to people because of previous negative experiences with conversations. If you can believe it, humans can develop a sort of "conversation PTS", or post-traumatic stress. This always makes me feel sad because the ones who pull away from having conversations find themselves in a detached and lonely world.

And yet this I know: we can learn to deal successfully with challenging conversations so we don't have to hide from future ones! It is possible, and it can make your world a better place..

To clear any confusion, this chapter is how to successfully deal with an unsuccessful conversation and *still* move forward with that relationship. This is another strong, vital, and empowering skill set I wish I had learned earlier in my life. I could have saved a lot of time, energy, and heartache. I want others not to have to learn too late in their lives. Being resilient is a way to spring back to a full and productive life when we have been sidelined by a certain conversation.

Learning to Be Resilient

So, how do we become resilient in conversations?

First, we start by acquiring foundational skills (some of which we have already talked about in previous chapters). These are the vital, basic skills in having conversations; we just don't learn them. We simply assume we know them because we know how to talk.

1. **Choose Resilience by Being Responsible for Your Own Emotions:** A must-have skill for being resilient is being responsible for our feelings and emotions. Growing up, we may have been taught a lot about responsibilities but not so much about being responsible for how we *feel*. In school, we learn all the essentials of IQ (intelligence quotient), solving math problems, and learning biology, but not EQ (emotional quotient). We were told, "Just be happy anyway," or "Learn to deal with it." The problem is that life skills were only learned as we tried to progress forward in life with other emotionally hindered people. Learn-as-you-go type of teaching. What happens with that is if we never learn, we never stop destroying relationships, including the one with ourselves. We could switch that around to learn and go.

2. **Be Resilient in Knowing Your Role and Stay the Course:** As my kids got older, I found that conversations got harder because they were choosing many more things, including emotions and behaviors for themselves, and I was no longer in charge. Mind you, my problem, not theirs. I could either fail at those vital conversations, or I could choose to be resilient by choosing better emotions for myself about the changes that were happening. After taking responsibility for my own emotions and moving forward with better conversations, the fact that they had a right to their own lives was central to understanding my role. It was not their job to carry around their mother's emotions! The journey of my kids growing into adulthood challenged me, and I could either remain stuck because of my emotions or be resilient. While not perfect, I now choose better emotions for myself, which helps me actually *enjoy* even our difficult conversations now.

3. **Being Resilient by Learning How to Apologize:** Have you asked yourself why apologizing is so hard, perhaps even excruciating? For some folks, it's not, but for most of us, apologizing is difficult to say the least. We have been fed falsehoods about apologizing, that it's a sign of weakness, and we will lose the respect of others if we admit we were wrong. Often, we simply were not shown any examples of people admitting they made a mistake! Here we go again! Parents, spouses, teachers, leaders, and others need to step up and be an example and embrace apologizing when necessary. Mistakes made and not acknowledged can affect generations in families and societies, with a

detrimental effect when families cling to cultures of being right no matter what. Clans, societies, and even countries have gone to war, killing thousands-even millions-because someone had to have it their way.

Apologizing has many more tremendous benefits than we have been led to believe. It could be the catalyst for deep profound healing in relationships. As you get better at Purple CHATs, you will know when to apologize because your heart will tell you. I call it "Wisdom of the Heart."

4. **Choose Resilience in Not Taking Things Personally:** As a real estate agent, I encounter difficult conversations all the time. The business of real estate involves a lot of money, deadlines, decisions, and emotions, all revolving around people's lives. Sometimes problems arise in the middle of transactions. People get upset. Clients have certainly said things to me in these stressful situations that are not easy to hear. Such conversations can become uncomfortable. Even then, I have *choices*. I can react defensively and make the situation worse, or I can stay grounded, not take things personally and focus on solving the problem. This can be done when you are secure enough inside yourself that you don't have to take on someone else's emotions. That is being resilient. I have had to be accepting of how clients feel, while at the same time choosing not to be defensive. Tough conversations show everybody's true colors. I try to be aware of what color *I* am manifesting..

5. **Resilience Means to Keep Trying:** When having tough conversations, keep going! This doesn't mean doing the same thing over and over, expecting different results (insanity). It means to keep trying but in a *different* way so that the tough conversation eventually becomes easier. Try again by thinking differently about the message, be calmer, listen more, or use different words.

While working at a doctor's office, at the beginning of my Purple CHATS journey, one of my jobs was to collect on patients' overdue balances. Believe me, it was not fun. Who wants someone calling them about money they owe? I was miserable. Instead of giving up, I decided to try a different approach, using different words. Experimenting until I found words and phrases that worked best, I discovered that better words and the right tone, coming from the heart, were a magical combination.

"Kill 'em with Kindness" was my mantra every time I picked up the phone. It worked! People stayed on the phone, and we worked out solutions together. Clients felt heard, seen, and made their payments. It was powerful!

By learning how to be resilient, I was part of the *solution* instead of the problem. I loved the results.

To make it easy to remember, here are five ways to be resilient in your conversations:

1. Take responsibility for your own emotions. (I know I have said that before.)
2. Know your role in the conversation. (Sort through the mess.)
3. Apologize when you should. (You'll know when.)
4. Don't take things personally. (Stick with the message.)
5. Try again; don't give up. (Keep showing up.)

This is not a comprehensive list of how to be resilient. These are starters. You will be the best at being resilient if you spend time and energy figuring out for yourself what works for you. Create your own path on how to be resilient! Remember it's your responsibility, not the world around you, on how you handle your conversations.

The Mental Health Purple Chat

There's one last kind of resiliency, and honestly, it might be the most powerful. I call it **Resiliency at Its Best**. These are the conversations that require more from us than just words—they need our heart. This kind of resiliency shows up when we keep coming back to the same difficult conversation, not because we enjoy it, but because we care. We don't run from the discomfort. We come back—again and again—to show the other person, *"I'm here. I care. And I'm not giving up on this or on you."*

It's not easy. In fact, it's really hard. But when we keep showing up with compassion and a willingness to listen, it can lead to real understanding, healing, and even life-changing results.

The conversations I'm talking about involve someone with mental health struggles. It does not include abusive, harmful communication. These struggles I am talking about might include depression, anxiety, addiction, loss, dementia, obsessive behavior, or trauma of some kind. Life brings all of us mental health challenges to some degree or another, so it's in all of our best interest that there is no "us versus them." We are *all* struggling with imperfect bodies and brains.

For some, these struggles are manageable, but for others the struggles might consume and dictate their everyday lives. I bet we all know someone who is dealing with a mental health challenge. These struggles are real. It's time we hug them and ask how we can help, instead of blaming, shaming, or hindering. Let's talk about what's not being talked about.

Conversations about mental health struggles are challenging. Most people experiencing issues *want* to talk about them' they just don't know how. Mental health is complicated, and one size does not fit all. I have been involved with people, including family members, who have experienced all kinds of life-altering health struggles. These struggles can divide people and hurt and destroy relationships. It's painful to go through them and especially difficult to watch. While it's impossible to handle these interactions perfectly, a better way is possible.

Beyond Allowing Isolation: The Power of Resilience

When my husband and I had a young family, my sister Heather and her husband Rob had two boys the same age as our kids. We didn't live in the same town, but close enough that we got together to do activities as families. Their oldest boy, Coleman, at the age of ten, started to develop some real, unrelenting challenges of depression, anxiety, OCD, anorexia, and more. While it was painful for my family to watch, for Coleman's parents, it was excruciating. Despite trying every solution possible, there was no relief that came. At one point, my sister said she had been to the depths of hell.

This family's experience over a full decade made them feel lonely, isolated, different, and hopeless. Most of the time, they felt like no one understood and no one could help them. And it was true–unless you are the one going through it, you can't understand. They were often further victimized by uncomfortable conversations that were blunt, raw, and sometimes offensive. They had times of barely hanging on.

Many times, Heather and Rob pushed away, isolating themselves. Somehow (with God's help), I knew that through all the painstaking conversations, they needed people to *stay* with them, not desert them.

During a time when things were really bad, I had one of these raw, uncomfortable conversations with my brother-in-law. Coleman had been in and out of the hospital, and they had concluded that this was how life was going to be. We were having this conversation in a house full of family members and literally chaos, with little kids running around. I remained focused on our conversation.

"I will be here and will do whatever I can, even if that means carrying him to the hospital myself."

"Thanks, but no thanks," Rob said wryly. "People say things like this all the time, but they really don't mean it." His head shifted position, but his voice steadied. "When it gets really hard, they don't show up."

I couldn't excuse other people's behavior, but I knew I wasn't leaving the conversation.

"I'm not like other people. If you can't continue the day-to-day battle, I am ready to step in and do it for you."

Despite all the confusion and noise, I kept my eyes focused on him. Finally, I saw his eyes soften as he could tell that I was not giving up; I was letting him know that there was nothing he could say that would make me disappear. I knew the more resilient I could become, the more help I could give.

This experience taught me about caring enough to come back to tough conversations again and again with your heart and your presence, and with a lot of prayers.

Coleman peacefully passed away at the age of twenty-two at his parents' home. He was a great soul. He blessed my life in ways that nobody else could. I will be forever grateful that I chose to show up for him and his family. I love and adore this family, and we continue to have Purple CHATs.

Staying Steadfast

Years passed, and then one day, I met Sandy. I was sitting alone at church one day when Sandy—who hadn't been to church in quite some time—felt a pull to attend. Though the back rows had plenty of open seats where she could have quietly slipped in, this beautiful blonde woman walked confidently down the aisle, fully visible to the congregation, and sat right next to me. That simple act turned into the beginning of a meaningful friendship. Sandy and I connected quickly. She opened up about her life—serious health struggles, depression, and deep emotional pain from two difficult marriages. I told her, "I'm here as a friend, and

I'll help however I can." And I meant it. We shared honest conversations and moments of encouragement. But sometimes, her pain would get in the way. She'd cancel plans, avoid my calls, or pull away in ways that hurt. When that happened, I'd pause and ask myself, *What if that was one of my family members? What if I were the one struggling like that?* Those questions softened my heart. They reminded me not to take her behavior personally. Her actions weren't a rejection of me; they were a reflection of the battle she was fighting inside.

Eventually, after we weathered those ups and downs, Sandy admitted how deeply she regretted the times she pulled away. But what mattered most is that we stayed in the conversation. I kept coming back—not perfectly, but with grace—and that's what built the trust we share now.

Today, she's the kind of friend who will show up for me too, especially when *my* life hits a few bumps. I'm grateful not only for her friendship but also for what God showed me through our journey: that real connection happens when we choose compassion over offense, presence over withdrawal, and grace over pride.

Having had these experiences and others, I learned the following when dealing with deeply challenging conversations:

1. Resist the temptation to be offended.
2. Listen more and better.
3. Care deeply with your heart and especially with your presence.

Why Is Being Resilient Important?

Not all difficult conversations will be resolved in the first attempt. To keep trying is courageous. Even then, some conversations will not be resolved. To recognize that is part of being honest. And it's also thoughtful to know when not to have a conversation and just be present, especially when the pain is great. But resolved or not, the conversation that says "I care no matter what happens" is a resilient one. It takes lots of heart when things are difficult to just be present. And remember, being present is a conversation in and of itself.

Purple CHAT Questions:

1. How am I doing at being resilient in my conversations?
2. Do I take things personally and leave the conversation?
3. Who do I have conversations with that require resiliency, at its best?

18

Regret or Rejoice: Your Choice

"Success is the sum of small efforts,
repeated day in and day out."
—Robert Collier

There I was, standing on the porch with great anticipation, waiting for the front door to open. *This day has finally come!* On the other side of the door were two of my best friends whom I had not seen in over thirty years. We had all lived together in an apartment in our early twenties. Despite all being from very different places, we became friends fast. Instant friends.

Tammy grew up in Hawaii and was so kind; Hoda was from England and had a darling accent; and I, an Arizona girl ready for adventure. Boy, did we have them!

Then, life happened, and we lost track of each other. Tammy, who ended up back in Hawaii, somehow found me one day through modern technology. Together, we searched for Hoda with so much excitement. Plans were made, and now it was time to meet at Hoda's house and my heart was pounding.

The door opened. "AHHH!" we all screamed, like you do when riding a roller coaster. Then it was hugs, more hugs, laughing, giggling, and I think we might have even jumped up and down. I felt like a little kid at Christmas. There was so much rejoicing in that house that we could have burst, just like old times!

What makes you rejoice, shout hallelujah, give a high five, or do a dance?

- When you reach a goal that stretches you beyond what you thought you could do.
- When you are surprised that you have money in your bank account at the end of the month.

- When you finally get a taste of that treat you have been craving for days.
- When you play the piano piece perfectly for the first time.
- When the yard looks great after you've sweated your guts out.
- When you go on that long-awaited vacation that you saved up for.
- When your favorite sports team came from behind and won at the last second.

Now I have to ask, do your conversations make you want to dance and shout with joy? Have you ever experienced a conversation where you walked away and exclaimed, "Yes! That was awesome!."

Or just maybe you say things like:

"I can't believe I said that. That went so bad!"

"Yes, I proved my point. I showed him! But now I feel bad."

"I have no idea what she was trying to say."

"He does all the talking. He doesn't even care what I think."

"I hate talking to people!"

I think most of us have said or thought of one of those phrases at some point. Some of us might even repeat them to ourselves daily. And let's be honest—those kinds of thoughts don't exactly lift our spirits. They often reflect feelings of frustration, anger, defensiveness, anxiety, confusion, or just plain irritation after a conversation.

But conversations don't have to leave us feeling that way. While they can be challenging, our mindset, our approach, and how we respond can make a big difference in how we feel afterward. It's normal to experience negative emotions—we're human. But if we routinely walk away from conversations feeling upset or drained, that pattern can lead to unhappiness over time.

It's no wonder so many people say they dread having conversations.

The question is, are we going to keep feeling negative after conversations, or can we change conversations around and handle them in such a way that we can say, "Yes! That was really good." As Chris Grosser says, "Opportunities don't happen, you create them."

Maybe you can relate to some of the following feel-good moments.

"Wow, she is really helpful."

"He likes to do the same things I do."

"Yay, my son did a good job today!"

"Hey, they want to get together with us!" and

"Great! Thanks for the cool idea!"

Now take that feeling of "Yes! That feels good," and see if that is happening in the most *important* conversations in your life. Do you get that feeling after talking to your boss about the upcoming deadline? Do you get that feeling after talking to your teenager about staying out late? How about talking to your spouse about finances? How do you feel when you talk to the neighbor that you don't know very well, your child's teacher, or the person next to you in a long line? And the big question, do you get that feel-good feeling after talking to yourself?

I will never forget the rejoicing feeling I had with my friend Caroline as we stood out on my driveway one evening chatting way too long. Before she got in her car, she said to me, "I have learned to love myself and I know that I have value."

I gasped with excitement, threw my arms around her, and basked in the overwhelming love I had for her and her journey. I sure wanted to do a celebration dance in the driveway, but I didn't. I just hugged her longer. After she left, I floated back into the house and was overcome with emotion at how Purple CHATS had changed her life and mine too. I had a heart full of gratitude for sure, and I knew God had also been part of this journey. I was so happy for her!

Learning to Turn This Joy Inward

I've come to realize how important it is to pay attention to how you speak to yourself and how those words make you feel. While writing this book, I battled with negative thoughts telling me to give up. One day, I decided to stop, and out loud, I told myself, "Dezlee, you're awesome." After being a little taken aback by my own words, I couldn't help but notice the wave of positive energy that washed over me. It felt amazing! While I've learned that my happiness is in my hands, I recognized that I'm never done practicing using positive, uplifting words with myself.

Oh, if we could only see ourselves as God sees us. Because He is the Almighty and sees things beyond our limited vision, He can help us find joy that comes from within if we will let Him in.

Why Is Feeling Good Important?

Heartfelt connections are never one-sided. When we truly speak from the heart, we naturally care about how the person on the other side of the conversation feels too. We shouldn't walk away from an interaction feeling good if our words have caused someone else pain. Real

connection grows from conversations that build trust—ones that help both people feel seen, valued, and uplifted.

When we strive to create positive, uplifting conversations, everyone benefits. It truly works. Every time you have a meaningful, heartwarming exchange, celebrate it. And then go and have another.

Purple CHAT Questions:

1. Do my conversations make me feel like rejoicing?
2. Am I helping others to have feel-good conversations?
3. What is one conversation I want to feel better about?

Oh, The Places You'll Go

"I am only one, but I am one. I cannot do
everything, but I can do something.
And I will not let what I cannot do
interfere with what I can do."
—Edward Everett Hale

There are moments in our lives that matter, and then there are those defining moments that truly shape us. More often than we realize, it's the conversations we have during these times that hold the greatest power. Some of the most dramatic shifts in my life began with just a few words—some uplifting, others painful. What I've learned is this, it's not just what words we're spoken, but how we choose to internalize and respond to those interactions that will ultimately determine our ability to create meaningful, powerful exchanges that bring about growth and connection to move us forward.

I will be forever grateful for a conversation I had as a young girl, a conversation that wasn't easy, but one that changed everything. It taught me that I am responsible for my own happiness. I learned not to wait for happiness to find me but to cultivate it from within. That moment became a constant light in my life, guiding me toward a life I truly love. Through deep soul work—and witnessing others do the same—I've come to see that heartfelt connections bring the most joy.

Please remember this: *Heartfelt Connections* is not about having perfect conversations; it's about having better ones, the kind that build bridges instead of walls. It's not about pretending the chaos and confusion of life don't exist but about recognizing that meaningful dialogue can make a difference despite all of it. There is no one-size-fits-all way to connect. We don't need everyone to be the same. No one else can be you. No one else can have the same influence you have or do the same good that only you can do. So start with you. Be You. Go out and connect your heart; the world needs you!

There's a verse in the Bible that says, "To everything there is a season, and a time to every purpose under heaven," (Ecclesiastes 3:1). Seasons and purpose are both essential to living fully. True living means embracing the season you're in right now, rather than spending all your energy waiting for the next one.

New seasons will come. New conversations will unfold. When your heart is connected to both yourself and to God, you are led into the seasons and purposes meant for your life.

It begins with honest conversations with yourself, making space within for what matters most. Only then can you create room for those meaningful seasons and purposes with the people you love most.

Because here's the truth; you don't want to miss those beautiful, once-in-a-lifetime opportunities.

There are countless kinds of conversations, and just as many books written about them. *Heartfelt Connections,* however, comes from a deeper place—a place of true connection.

It is fascinating that science continues to reveal what many of us don't take the time to fully understand, that our health and well-being are profoundly influenced by the quality of our relationships. And I can't say it enough that the relationship with yourself is the foundation on which all other relationships will be built on. Make your foundation strong and loving and others will be drawn to it. Love comes from respect, value, care, and appreciation. This is meant for you as well as others. Though not fully understood, there is something powerful—even mysterious—about genuine love and caring.

Real joy, and even better, health, seems to flow more freely when we take the time to truly connect. It isn't complicated. It simply starts with offering more of our hearts.

Not everyone we meet will be open to connection and that's okay. What matters is that we extend a helping hand and a loving heart. Because sometimes, just the *offer* of connection can make all the difference. And though we may never see the full impact, the effect can be deeper and more life-changing than we could ever imagine.

When I think of speaking words from the heart, the song "say love" by Hilary Weeks comes to mind:

> *A picture might be worth a thousand words*
> *But a heart can be changed by one*
> *Lives are shaped and minds are changed*

By what is said or what is not
There is a shortage in this world of "I believe in you"
And somebody, somewhere needs some.

Who doesn't need a kind word? I have yet to run into someone who says, "Don't be kind to me." What I have encountered while being on my journey of intentional connection is, "Oh, you are so kind!" like they are surprised at the kindness. I am always taken aback by this and say to myself after looking around, "Are people not kind? Is this a new concept?"

What I've come to realize is that there's a difference between being nice and being kind. Being nice and polite is wonderful—we could all use more of that—but kindness goes deeper. Kindness comes from the heart, not just from our words or manners. Too often, society mistakes kindness for weakness or a lack of ambition or intelligence. But the truth is, it takes far more inner strength, patience, integrity, and self-mastery to live with kindness than it ever does to live with contention.

Words are nice; hearts are kind.

So, a kind word is something spoken from the heart. There is a difference, and we all know it. Here are a few more words from the same song by Hilary Weeks:

We all give words away
Doesn't cost anyone a dime
But everyone knows there's a price to be paid
When the words are something less than kind

Deep down inside, we all want to be good and do good. Come and partake of the goodness that is in you. C. S. Lewis once said, "Good and evil both increase at compound interest. That is why the little decisions you and I make every day are of such infinite importance."

Don't wait. When you have an impression to connect, just do it! Be Heart Bold! Go out and create the color of purple by connecting your heart with other hearts. Humanity needs connection. It's how we can overcome all those issues that challenge us, and not only survive but thrive. Show the world that you have room to love and value others because you are loved and valued. Start the compounding interest one conversation at a time.

I see people all around me who are struggling with themselves, life, and relationships. Those struggles are real. I want to put my arms around them and give them hope and tell them it can be better, and you don't have to have money, more time, a certain job, or be a certain weight. It only requires more heart and better words. I hope you will go out and do the same for someone you know who needs a helping hand and a caring heart.

Having engaged in these powerful conversations for decades, I am thrilled to see the transformations people have made to create the life they want. They have found their value and can't help but see the value of humanity around them. Hearts are being healed and bridges are being built. Purple CHATs bring about a level of heightened awareness that broadens your world.

Now that you've learned the four steps to *Heartfelt Connections*—**a better you, a better message, better words, and showing up better**—I hope you'll begin applying them in your everyday conversations. It all comes down to your intentions and your choices. Each chapter was designed to help you grow in a specific way, and with practice, those changes will begin to take root. Don't feel like you have to master everything at once—start with the chapter that speaks to you most, and let it guide you forward.

If I were to simplify this entire book into one message, it would be this:

Learn to like yourself and take responsibility for your own happiness.

When you do that, everything else in life becomes easier.

As you practice the skills and insights from this book, you'll begin to discover a place within yourself that's open to receiving all that is good. Life will start to feel more vibrant, more connected, and you'll notice beauty and meaning in ways you never have before.

A friend once said to me after years of struggling, "I can't believe all the things I notice as I drive to work now. I have driven the same way so many times, but now I see the beauty that has been there the whole time!"

I hope you are experiencing this same thing as you have been making changes. Do you see people smile more because you smile? Do the words in a song that you have heard your whole life mean more to you because you listen differently? Does the sky seem bluer and the sunset more brilliant? Do you see the struggling mother at the grocery store or the older gentleman battling Parkinson's as he carries his food, and do you find a way to help? Do you feel more peace in your soul and recognize it as a blessing from God?

Life is so abundant. It's a gift to each of us, individually wrapped by the hands of the Almighty. Open it, look at it, marvel at it, and go and enjoy it. You will indeed find what you are looking for. Look, don't just wish for goodness, love, laughter, and beauty. They are there; don't miss them.

There is a term called "The Overview Effect." It's used to describe an experience the astronauts have when in space, looking back at planet Earth. It is a profound sense of awe along with an overwhelming appreciation for the Earth and mankind. This view of looking at the bigger picture causes a significant psychological shift in their understanding of how things are interconnected and a powerful realization of what is of greatest importance.

I invite you to experience The Overview Effect in your own life by gaining a transformative shift in how you view yourself, God, and humanity through your courageous, honest, and thoughtful conversations. The astronauts' experience happened above the Earth, while ours is taking place right amongst life itself on Earth. This overview is "The Life-View Effect." It's spectacular if you are willing to see the views. The Life-View Effect is zooming out from our day-to-day experiences, while looking through a different lens, so we can view our bigger story. This book has given you the skills to do exactly that; now it's up to you to choose.

Now that you can see yourself as an integral part of your own story, you can also recognize that you are indispensable. When you invite God into your view, His light expands your perspective and leads you beyond yourself—to see, feel, and celebrate the goodness of a divine power at work in your life. Including God in your picture enriches everything, allowing you to see all of humanity as part of the greater story you are privileged to live.

You are part of a grand scope of humanity that is connected in so many ways. You not only have a part in it, but most importantly, you have a responsibility to it. You now have the skills to courageously, honestly, and thoughtfully contribute to the care of humanity. Rise above your individual view and bask in The Life View because I promise you, it is spectacular.

I have been amazed at the places my journey has taken me. Not geographically, but with people and relationships. One Purple CHAT has taken me to another and another. I have found beautiful, heart-warming places and hope to continue to find more, and I know you will too.

I can't help but think of the book by Dr. Seuss, *Oh, the Places You'll Go*. Life does not have to be complicated because, "You have brains in your head, You have feet in your shoes, You can steer yourself any direction you choose." Choose to have heartfelt connections, and you will be amazed at the places you'll go. Your good and best life awaits!

It's Not the End

Writing this book has been one of the most unexpected and beautiful blessings of my life. I truly hope it has brought something meaningful to you as well. To walk this path with you—even across the pages—has been more than I ever dreamed possible.

Just when I think I've said everything I know about Purple CHATs, life surprises me. A new story unfolds, a new person enters, or a familiar truth deepens. It's been difficult to know where to place the final period because this journey keeps evolving. Even now, as I write this conclusion, my heart and hand say, *Wait! There's still one more thing to say!* So, let me say this: It's not the end. It's just the beginning!

I love conversations—have I mentioned that? I would *love* to hear about yours. How has your life shifted as you've begun using the principles presented in this book? What have you discovered about yourself, about others? What moments have challenged you, and which ones were magical?

And here's the question closest to my heart:

Do you love yourself?

If you would like to share, I would be honored to hear your story. You can reach out to me at <u>dezleehancock.com</u>

Thank you for reading, and for your heart.

With all my heart,
—Dezlee

Acknowledgements

After writing a book about connecting hearts, I am so grateful for every single heart that I've encountered. Life is a constant journey of amazement.

My life has been deeply enriched by my husband and children, who took this journey with me. They are my reasons for wanting better conversations. Clark, who has always been there even through the messes, but at times wondered if this book would ever get done. Wes, who kept me grounded by helping me see life through different lenses in our conversations. Karlie, who sparked my pursuit of better conversations. Abbey, my Purple CHATs partner in crime. I loved everything we learned together and still learning. And Lacey, for the blood, sweat, tears, and laughter through your hard journeys that lead to heartfelt connections.

I love you all!

Cindy Clemens was my first book mentor who took me by the hand and helped me believe in myself. She passed away from her fight with cancer before I got my first draft done and I didn't know what I was going to do. I found Caroll Shreeve, who kindly led me farther down the writer's path. I had many others who took me under their wing and truly wanted the best for me including Teresa Ford, Trina Boice, and AJ Jepperson with Eschler Editing. My final landing spot was with Bridget Cook Burch with Your Inspired Story. She has so much heart and vision that she knew exactly what to do with me and my book. I am beyond grateful! And then the ones who got it off the ground and made it take flight were Wendy Bates at BWW and Rebecca Hall Gruyter with Your Purpose Driven Practice. You made my dream come true. Thank you for your hearts!

Thank you to family members and others who put time and effort into reading and giving feedback. Matthew Seamons, Betsy Seamons, Heather Quist, Sharanette Farnsworth, Abbey Sawyer, Lacey Hancock, Karen Munson, Sonya Watkins, and Avalene Rumsey. Your efforts meant the world to me.

Besides those already mentioned, I had other cheerleaders who would not let me forget that I had a book to write. I will forever be grateful for their heartfelt encouragement. Sherrie Welch, Jill Demille, Carol Bergin, Sharley Funk, Becky Schmidt, Mindy Langford, and Shaun Stirland. If my mind has forgotten anyone, please know that my heart remembers.

About the Author

Dezlee Hancock is a communication advocate who believes deeply in the power of words—and even more in the power of meaningful conversation. She specializes in helping people reconnect with others and with themselves through honest, heartfelt dialogue that fosters clarity, compassion, and understanding.

An author, entrepreneur, mother, grandmother, and wife, Dezlee understands firsthand that every meaningful role in life requires next-level communication. In her debut book, *Heartfelt Connections*, she introduces the four essential elements for building—or rebuilding—healthy communication channels, offering a practical and hopeful path toward authentic connection and human flourishing.

Dezlee holds a degree in Human Communication, but she often says her most valuable education came from living a full, sometimes messy, always meaningful life. She believes every interaction carries the potential for love, learning, and laughter, and she thrives on genuine connection with the people she meets each day.

She also believes our world doesn't need more things—it needs more of what truly matters: people, hearts, and connection. These, she says, are the longest-lasting treasures we will ever have.

No stranger to being a little different, Dezlee embraces her quirks—from her unusual name and left-handedness to her love of weeding, unapologetic enjoyment of beets, and her tendency to savor deep conversations the way others savor dessert.

Her faith and family are her highest priorities. Dezlee is married to Clark, and together they have four children and three grandchildren—with hopes of welcoming more.

dezleehancock.com
dezleeh@gmail.com
https://www.facebook.com/dezlee.hancock

Book Reviews

Have you ever read a book and felt your whole life shift? Heartfelt Connections is that book! After studying human behavior for over thirty-five years, it's rare that I find a book about personal development that really moves me. Dezlee has created something truly soul-filling in the pages of this book. Her unique way of helping you really connect with yourself and then be equipped to honestly connect with others is nothing short of powerful. The real-life stories she shares, the practical 'Purple Heart' questions she asks, and the guided 'How-To' steps she offers are nothing short of pivotal. I can't wait to share this book with everyone I know and love! Thank you for sharing your beautiful heart, Dezlee.

—Laurie Hartley-Moore, Holistic Health Practitioner

Heartfelt Connections is a beautifully written, deeply sincere guide to creating conversations that heal, uplift, and transform. As I read, I repeatedly found myself in these stories—seeing my own habits, hopes, and struggles reflected with compassion. Those moments made me realize that real change is possible. The lessons and lived experiences shared here gently invite you to take constructive steps toward the life you want and the relationships that truly nourish you. With spiritual insight and practical guidance, this book becomes a warm companion, showing how courageous, honest, and thoughtful words can reshape your world from the inside out.

—Gary L. Fretwell, #1 International Best-selling Author of: *The Magic of a Moment: Unlock the Potential in Every Moment* and *Unlocking the Magic: Your Daily Journal*

Reading this book feels like I am sitting down with my long-lost friend Dezlee. Her words are invitations to creating a lifelong love story with one's self, as well as creating more meaningful relationships with those in your world. Every chapter begins with inspiring quotes and ends with self-reflection questions. Heartfelt Connections is a journey and a conversation that I want to return to over and over again as the author reminds us, practice makes better. Her written

voice is warm and full of compassion as she walks with us through her own experiences and vulnerabilities, and then invites us to share and reflect upon our own. This book is a gift of love.
—Sherry Lynn Campbell, Novelist, Children's Author and Storyteller, WonderEddy.com

Heartfelt Connections by Dezlee is a luminous exploration of love, loss, and the invisible threads that bind us. With poetic honesty and emotional depth, Dezlee invites readers into moments of raw humanity and spiritual awakening. Every page feels like a mirror reflecting both vulnerability and strength. This is a beautifully written, soul-nourishing book that lingers long after the final page. I loved her conversations about resiliency. Her examples from her own family issues were truly inspiring and heartfelt. I could not put the book down. This is an example of truth and raw emotion that inspired me from the depths of my heart!
—Deborah Wiener, Author, Speaker, Business Consultant, and Coach, Deborah@DeborahWiener.com

At some point in our lives, we will be faced with difficult conversations, either with family members, professionals, or both. This book provides great insight and tools to help in those times. I began applying these recommendations as soon as I read them. I now try to see things from the other person's perspective, and it's really helped me resolve conflicts in a way that leaves me feeling better whether I'm in the wrong or have been wronged.
This is a book I will keep close by and reflect on often. I highly recommend!
—Wendy L Hooton- Author, *Big People Don't Pee in the Park: A Mother and Son's Journey with Down Syndrome*, Down Syndrome Advocate, Speaker. wendyhooton.com

Everyone can benefit from Heartfelt Connections. Dezlee's insights and experiences with a better way of communicating will change your life. She leads you through exercises that will empower you to show up with courage, honesty, and thoughtfulness. Take the challenge and watch the relationship with yourself and others turn into meaningful bonds that add depth and joy to your life.
—Betsy Seamons, LCSW

This book is empowering and impressive!

Heartfelt Connections discusses conversations we have within ourselves that are so abundant. It is vitally important that we intentionally mind what we say internally so that we can connect with ourselves in the truest sense. Connecting with ourselves gives us the ability to make and keep healthy, authentic relationships with others. This book illuminates with clarity who has responsibility within our relationships and can help one navigate into heartfelt connections that have been difficult for years! Though we may have many difficult relationships to work on, this book is one of the best tools to create a positive outcome.

Heartfelt Connections is the worldview solution to coming together as a human race. If we can choose to go from quickly texting out of convenience to Purple CHAT conversations, we can heal our own disjointed world one willing heart at a time.

—Lisa Sitze, #1 International Best-selling Author of *Facing Your Demons*

For a self-help book, I found myself immediately drawn to Dezlee's passion and complete commitment to changing the serious breakdown in our society when it comes to communicating and showing respect for one another. I was pleasantly surprised as a person who isn't usually drawn to self-help books that I couldn't put it down in my first read.

I then picked it back up for a second time the very next day and read it again but this time wrote notes and found specific areas in my life that could use improvement. I am excited to implement some ideas she shares.

Today, I even used one of her examples with my husband and just simply took a greeting I give him most mornings and added just two words and had an extremely long, beautiful conversation with him that was comical and fun. I recommend this book for ANYONE. We all can use this book to break down our own barriers and improve our relationships with one Courageous,

Honest, and Thoughtful conversation at a time! The world needs Dezlee's book!

—Sanya Watkins, Writer, Story Coach, Inspired Writer

Upleveling your relationships

    Dezlee Hancock invites the reader to see conversations in a fresh, inspiring way that transforms communication. She makes a common practice of conversing an opportunity for understanding and real bonding. Since implementing her CHAT formula, I've seen a significant improvement in my ability to communicate more deeply with my family, making basic conversations more meaningful and effective. I was a little skeptical at first, wondering how a talk with my husband could improve that much, but it has. I recommend this book to everyone who wants to uplevel their relationships, whether at work, at home, or in the community.

—Karen Munson, Author of the *God Given Grit* series

Heartfelt Connections is a warm, spirit-centered guide to building better conversations from the inside out. Dezlee Hancock blends personal stories, faith, and emotional wisdom to show how deeply our communication shapes our relationships—and our joy. I loved how she returns again and again to the idea that everything begins with self-responsibility: knowing who we are, nurturing ourselves, and choosing how we show up. Her concept of "Purple CHATs" feels like a breath of fresh air in a world that desperately needs more courage, honesty, and thoughtfulness in how we speak to one another.

    What I appreciated most is that the book doesn't pretend conversations are easy. Dezlee acknowledges the messiness, the discomfort, and the emotional weight we carry into our interactions. Yet she offers a hopeful, doable path forward grounded in compassion, resilience, and an active relationship with God. This is the kind of book that reminds you of who you want to be—both for yourself and the people you love. It's heartfelt, practical, faith-anchored, and full of light.

—Lauri Mackey, Authoress of *Positivity Happens*

www.ingramcontent.com/pod-product-compliance
Lightning Source LLC
Chambersburg PA
CBHW021044130626
46552CB00005B/2009